# TOUCHDOWN AMERICA

Charleston, SC
www.PalmettoPublishing.com

*Touchdown America*
Copyright © 2023 by Robby Wells

Hardcover ISBN: 979-8-8229-1321-9
Paperback ISBN: 979-8-8229-1322-6
eBook ISBN: 979-8-8229-1323-3

R O B B Y   W E L L S

# TOUCHDOWN AMERICA

## FROM CHAMPION TO SHAME TO CONTENDER

# Contents

# Introduction

## December 17, 1988 – Pocatello, Idaho

"OK, HERE WE GO" coach Satterfield said as he looked at Franky Debusk, our starting quarterback. "I want North – Pro – Forty – Two – Lead on one." As Franky trotted to the huddle from the sideline, you could tell that something beyond all expectations was about to happen. Coach Satterfield was known for being a conservative play caller, and the first play of this game was no different. The play called was a basic running play to our running back, Dwight Sterling.

As Franky entered the huddle, he looked into the eyes of his teammates with a twinkle in his eye and said, "Hey guys! Time to make history! I want North – Pro – Forty – Two – Lead on one on one! Ready – Break!" The offensive players broke the huddle and hustled to the line to meet their opponent for the first time that night.

As Franky barked out the cadence, "Down – Blue – 16 – Blue – 16, Check – Check – Red - Ninety – Eight – Red – Ninety – Eight." There was not a safety in the middle of the field, and Franky had checked to a deep pass on the first play of the biggest game of our lives. "Set! Hit!" Franky took the ball from our All – American Center, Steve Dugan, and faked a running play that fooled the entire defense.

There was nobody in the middle of the field except one lone receiver named Donald Lipscomb from Gaffney, South Carolina. Franky threw the ball as far as he could, and it looked like he had overthrown Donald by a mile. Just then Donald turned on his jets, and just before the ball fell to the turf, he made a full speed dive stretching out as far as he possibly could manage. The ball dropped right into his hands. It was a fifty-eight yard pass that was completed on the first play of the 1988 I-AA National Championship game between Furman University and Georgia Southern University. The play set the tone for the entire night, and Furman went on to win the title by a score of 17 – 12. WE WERE CHAMPS! WE WERE THE BEST!

At the beginning of the season, we were picked to be seventh in the Southern Conference. That did not matter because we believed. I was just a walk-on football player. There was no athletic scholarship waiting on me when I arrived at Furman University, but my experience at Furman was priceless. Our team was comprised of young men from many different backgrounds and multiple ethnicities. We did not concern ourselves with how we were different. We focused on how we were the same. Great feats can be accomplished when everyone comes together with one single purpose.

# The Crimson Tide vs The Ole' Miss Rebels

I t was the fall of 1980, and I was a twelve year old kid growing up in 'L.A.' Now you may think that 'L.A.' means Los Angeles, but it actually means Lower Alabama. There was not even a traffic light in my home town, Clayton, Alabama. The population was less than a thousand people, and most of the people were farmers. Our town was so small that leaving your doors unlocked at night was a common practice. My father was the minister at the only Baptist Church in town, and my mother taught music lessons. When the farmers' crops were good, they would give to the church, and our family would do well. But when the crops were bad, things would get tough at home. I can remember the farmers strike back in the 70's. All of the local farmers drove their tractors through town in a parade protesting the federal policies that were causing them to go bankrupt. I was too young to understand all of the politics, but it was the most exciting thing we had ever seen in Clayton until a DC-3 was caught with $8 million worth of marijuana at our local airport. Our airport was small like the town, and the pilot of that DC-3 had to cut off two of the four engines in order to land on the short run way.

Whenever a plane would land in Clayton, the chief of police, or his one side kick would drive out and act as a taxi for the people flying in. You can just imagine the surprise of the drug smugglers when a police car showed up while they were unloading the plane. It made national news, and was the talk of the town for years.

My father had always wanted to fly, so he got his private pilot's license and flew any chance that he could get. My dad was, and still is my hero, and I wanted to fly with him whenever he took the small plane up.

In the state of Alabama, you have to devote your allegiance to The University of Alabama or to Auburn University. People take their football very serious, and to most it is a true religion. I am sure that people around the country would try to argue who has the fiercest rivalry, but there is no rivalry that can compare to Alabama and Auburn. For those who would argue against this statement, let me give you my reasoning. On several occasions, I witnessed my father giving marriage counseling to several different couples. Usually their feud would stem from one pulling for Alabama and one pulling for Auburn. I strongly doubt that any other rivalry has caused as many fist fights, divorces, or other crimes of passion.

Well, I chose to pull for the Crimson Tide because I have always loved a winner. Coach Bryant had a well oiled machine, and was always in the national championship hunt. Beating Auburn was expected, and usually the Crimson Tide would reign victorious over the Tigers.

Guice Slawson was the mayor of Louisville, Alabama, and a friend of my father. Mr. Slawson was an alum of The University of Alabama, and had flown with my dad on several trips around the state. I remember the day he called my dad and asked him if he would be willing to fly him to Tuscaloosa to see the Crimson Tide play the Ole' Miss Rebels. He had a couple of extra tickets, and said that I could come along for the ride.

This would be the first time that I would see the Crimson Tide play. The day was perfect. I was always excited to fly, and seeing the Crimson Tide play live was a major thrill for me. We arrived at Bryant-Denny Stadium fairly early, and I got to watch the teams warm up. Coach Bryant was leaning against the goal post during the warm-ups, and the atmosphere was electrifying. It was not a close game. Alabama destroyed Ole' Miss that day. It seemed like Alabama scored every time they had the ball in the first half.

We were sitting in the end zone and I remember telling my dad that I would like to do that one day. He looked at me and said, "What? You would like to play for Alabama one day?" I looked at him and said "No. I want to do that one day," as I pointed to Coach Bryant. A lot of the people sitting around us heard me, and began to chuckle. I remember that my dad looked at me and said, "If that is really what you want to do, then you can do it."

# Clayton Elementary

We moved to Clayton, Alabama when I was six years old. Desegregation had begun less than ten years before I started school, and a lot of the white people in the South decided to form private schools to educate their children separate from black children. Most of the white children in Clayton went to one of two private schools that were fairly close to town. Lakeside School was about thirty minutes away in Eufaula, Alabama, and the other private school was ten minutes away in Louisville, Alabama. The name of that school was Dixie Academy. It was a fitting name for the part of the country that we lived in. We truly were living in the Heart of Dixie.

My parents always taught me that all people were precious in God's sight, and that racism was wrong. My parents enrolled me in Clayton Elementary, the local public school. It was the right choice for my family, and besides, my father did not make enough to send me to a private school. There were not very many white children in the school. In fact, I can only recall about four other white students in that school. One of my closest friends was Anthony Settles. He was always smiling, and it never crossed our minds that we had different skin colors. I was friends with the few white students, but I was friends with all of the black children also.

Learning to relate at such a young age to people that looked different from me would prove to be very valuable to me in my personal and professional life. The life lessons that I learned were more important to my career than learning science, math, or any other subject that was taught in the classroom. It was the beginning of my preparation for a great career that I have cherished and loved. Attending Clayton Elementary School gave me a solid foundation that most people, black and white, can not understand.

When I was in the third grade, our class had just come back to school from Christmas break. My third grade teacher was Mrs. Horne. She was a great teacher, and her husband was the local veterinarian. Mrs. Horne stood in front of the class and asked each of us the same question. "What do you want to be when you grow up?" Well, you got a lot of the typical responses from most of the students. Most of the girls wanted to be nurses or school teachers. Most of the little boys wanted to be policemen and firemen. When she came to me, she asked the same question, but I gave her a different answer. "I want to be a college football player, win a national championship, and coach football. Then I want to be the President of the United States." Most of the students laughed because the very thought of me playing football seemed absurd. You see, I wore corrective shoes because my feet turned in. I was pigeon toed. Running was not possible because I would trip over my own feet. To my classmates, playing football seemed like an unobtainable goal for me.

Then again, maybe they laughed because I wanted to be the President of the United States. What most of my friends did not realize was that my family friend, Jimmy Carter, had just won the White House.

Well, my shoes began to work, and my legs got stronger. I began to run, and continued to run even to this day. When I entered high school, I played football. When I went to college, I played football. When I was a junior in college, we won the national championship. I was an educator and football coach for twenty years. Who is laughing now? Do I consider myself a success? Sure I do, but not because of the number of wins that I have under my belt. Successful people are winners because they have overcome adversity in their life. Show me a successful person in any field, and I will show you a person that has overcome the odds. As a child, my adversity was being pigeon toed. I overcame it. What is your adversity? Find a way to overcome it. Win!

# President Jimmy Carter

A beautiful young girl went away to college with all of her hopes and dreams ahead of her. Very quickly the students and faculty realized how talented this young girl was. Just as most young girls fall in love, this beautiful young girl fell in love, but the man was older and had a family. One thing led to another, and all of a sudden there was an unwanted pregnancy – a mistake. Her friends tried to tell her that it was just a blip on the radar. She was advised not to ruin her career by having the baby. At the last moment, that beautiful young girl went against the advice from her friends and decided to give the child a chance by putting the child up for adoption after the baby was born. I have always said that if I ever meet that beautiful young girl I will thank her for setting my life in motion. That beautiful young girl is my birth mom. In February of 2016 I met her for the first time.

I was adopted when I was six weeks old to a great family in Bartow, Georgia. My adopted mother had given birth nine years before I was born to my sister, Caryl Marie Wells. There were complications in my mother's pregnancy, and Caryl was born with several birth defects. She was born blind, partially deaf, and mentally challenged. Because of the complications during pregnancy, my mother could not have anymore children. They decided to adopt, and ended up getting me in the late spring of 1968. The adoption agency called me "Baby Andy." For 47 years I did not know who my birth parents were. Our family was given a brief history of my birth mom and birth dad, but that was all.

I have never had a huge desire to look for my birth parents because I had a great childhood, and had great adoptive parents. What would have been the point? I appreciate the fact that my mother chose to give birth instead of the other option. I am sure that it crossed her mind. If she had chosen the other option, I would not be here. I guess you could say that I am a miracle and one of the most unlikely to be here, but after many years of searching my birth mom found me. More to come later in the book.

We lived in the state of Georgia until I was ready to start elementary school. While we were living in Waynesboro, Georgia, my father was the minister of a local church. He also was on a state committee that focused on issues of special needs children. My dad had the chance to work with Jimmy Carter, who was the governor of Georgia at the time. I actually remember meeting Jimmy Carter at his inauguration as governor. I was just a young child, but it stuck in my mind. Just before Jimmy Carter won the office of President of the United States, our family moved to Clayton, Alabama. When I went to school the day after President Carter was elected, all of my classmates and teachers did not believe that I had met the President of the United States.

Clayton was a very small town, and my teachers actually called a conference with my parents because they thought that I was not telling the truth. Well, you can only imagine how awkward those teachers felt when my parents showed up for the meeting with a family picture with President Carter. I became an instant hero with all of my classmates.

The night that Jimmy Carter won the Whitehouse, I can remember sitting in front of the television set with the hopes that he would win. When all the votes were tallied, and Jimmy Carter had been declared the winner, I remember running around the house because I was so excited. That moment in time etched a spark of inspiration on my heart that I would one day run for and become the President of the United States. I was only eight years old, but the desire was there. It was strong, it was burning, and it was real.

# Midland Valley High School

M inisters move around to different churches every few years, and we had been in Clayton, Alabama for eight years. On the average, a Baptist minister moves about every four years. I guess my father went way over the average, but there came a time that my family decided to move. My father took a new church on the outskirts of Aiken, South Carolina in a small mill town called Graniteville. Most of my dad's church members had some sort of affiliation with the Graniteville Mill and Swint Mill. While we lived there, I attended Midland Valley High School. I started Midland Valley as a true ninth grader.

I decided that I was going to play football for the High School, and went to the school to meet the head football coach. His name was Reed Charpia. He had just taken the position. He had been the head coach at Newberry College, but wanted to coach his son, Rusty. Rusty was a junior, and a very cocky quarterback. It was ok that he was cocky because he could back it up. Rusty was a talented athlete. The school was only a couple of years old, so everything we did was basically the first time that it had been done there. I ended up playing tight end all four years of my high school career. Our practice field did not have any grass. We practiced in the sand. Imagine practicing football in the middle of August in a dust bowl. We must have truly wanted to play, if we were going to put ourselves through that punishment.

Our school had never had a stadium, much less a winning season. We played our home games in the outfield of a middle school baseball park. All of that changed my senior season. The new stadium had been finished and we had the chance to have a great season. I will never forget the first game that was played in our new stadium. We were playing Aiken High School. On the first play from scrimmage our running back, Jeff Tilby, scored on a 70 yard rush. We went on to win a very close game against the Green Hornets.

That was a very memorable season for several reasons. We went 8-4 that year for the first winning season in the history of the school. It was also the first time that we had been to the playoffs. Memories last a lifetime, and good memories become sweeter as the years go by. During that season, we played Greenwood High School at home. Greenwood was the number one team in the state of South Carolina, and sported a 7-0, undefeated record when they rolled into town. Their team was ranked #7 in the nation in the USA Today High School Poll. The chances of beating this team seemed absolutely ridiculous, but we believed.

Greenwood jumped out to a 14-0 lead in the first quarter, but Coach Charpia had coached us all week to stay calm. Once they went up by two touchdowns, Greenwood went flat. Our team realized what was going on, and we began to gain momentum. We scored just before half time, and Coach Charpia decided to go for two. We called time-out, and Coach told the ref to place the ball on the left hash. As we all huddled around our coach during the timeout, he said, "Let's run the Tight End Screen." Wait a minute. I was the Tight End! We had run that play every day in practice, but we had never run it in a game. On the play, I had to fall down when the ball was snapped, and act like I was lost on a slow trot. I remember breaking the huddle and getting in my stance on the left side of the line of scrimmage. It was a big game. It was a big play. My heart felt like it was going to beat out of my chest. Our center snapped the ball, and our quarterback, William Walker rolled out to his right. I fell to the ground, and all of the defense swarmed towards our quarterback. Just before he was hit by four Greenwood players, he turned back towards me and threw a touch pass. There was no one even close to me. I was all by myself. I kept thinking – "Catch it! Catch it!" Well, I did, and I trotted into the endzone untouched. It was a different game now. The score was 14-8, and we had the momentum. It was on!

We came out the second half and shut Greenwood down. We ended up winning the game by a score of 22-16, and we gave them the only two points they scored in the second half. We took a safety on purpose late in the game to keep from punting out of our own endzone.

I was never the best player on the team, but I studied the game, and worked extremely hard to give myself a chance at success. High School was great, but I wanted to play college football. I wanted to coach, and I knew that I would be able to learn a lot if I was given the chance to play on the next level.

# Furman University

I fell in love with Furman University when I was a junior in high school. It was the fall of my junior year at Midland Valley and Furman was celebrating youth day during their game against Davidson College. Furman demolished Davidson, and I liked the fact that the Paladins knew how to win. That was important to me. I also liked the campus. The school was considered to be the hardest school academically in the state of South Carolina, and the student population was only 2,500. The deciding factor for me was not the academics, or the football program. What truly sold me on Furman was being able to feed the ducks on Furman Lake after the football game that day. I am sure that plenty of potential student – athletes decide to go to Furman because of Furman Lake and the ducks that live there. I also wanted to go to a school that had a strong winning tradition because I knew that I would be able to learn a lot about coaching. I was a realist as a player. I knew my limitations as an athlete, and I wanted to learn coaching strategies and techniques from a great coaching staff. It was a great fit for me.

When I was a senior in high school, Furman played for the national championship in Tocoma, Washington against Georgia Southern. The entire first half was all Furman, and it appeared that the school I was about to attend was going to win the national championship. Obviously Irk Russell, the head coach for Georgia Southern, and their starting quarterback, Tracy Ham, had different plans. The entire second half belonged to Georgia Southern, and with only a few seconds left in the game, Tracy Ham threw a winning touchdown pass to beat Furman for the 1985 I-AA National Championship.

I knew that it would leave a bad taste in the mouths of the returning Furman players. I also knew that Furman would have a chance to win another title within the next few years. It was an easy choice for me. I chose to walk – on the football team as a true freshman in the fall on 1986. The Furman program was going through some major changes when I arrived. The head coach, Dick Sheridan, had just left to take the head coaching job at North Carolina State University. His Furman teams had beaten the Wolfpack two times, and their administration decided that they could not beat Coach Sheridan, so they had better hire him.

The new head coach at Furman was Jimmy Satterfield. He was an offensive mind, and had been the offensive coordinator for several years. It was a great promotion for him, and it kept some continuity in the program. Coach Satterfield was an expert on option football, and there were several schools that tried to hire him away from Furman. Right after the 1985 national title game, Lou Holtz talked with Coach Satterfield about being the offensive coordinator at Notre Dame.

Coach Satterfield decided to take the head job at Furman, and his first year as head coach was my first year at Furman. It did not take me long to realize that everyone on the team was bigger, faster, and stronger than my old high school teammates. I was going to have to work extremely hard to have a chance. I was going to have to work just as hard in the classroom to graduate from Furman.

I had several roommates during my four years at Furman. My freshman year, I roomed with a 5'7" kicker from Lugoff, South Carolina. His name was Mike Wood. Mike did not look like a football player, but he was very strong, and he could kick. As a true freshman, in the first game of the season, Mike set a school record for making the longest field goal against South Carolina State University. It was a 52 yard field goal, but it would have been good from 62 yards. His leg was extremely strong and accurate. In his second game, he hit a field goal late in the game to tie Bill Curry's Georgia Tech team 17 – 17 in Atlanta, Georgia. We were a much smaller school than Georgia Tech, and the headlines of the Sunday paper read "Furman Wins 17-17."

During my senior year, I roomed with our starting free safety, Will Hall. Will was tall and lanky, but he could play the game. After we graduated, Will coached for a while at Buford High School in North Georgia. A lot of former Furman football players have gone on to coach. Today Will is working overseas in Kuwait with another former Furman football player named Pat Turner. They are running a fitness facility and doing extremely well. I was very close to Will and Pat. They were great guys. They had my back, and I had theirs. They did not look like me, but we did not care. I was white. They were black. It did not matter that our skin was different colors because we all wore purple and white. We were brothers.

Our country would do well to study how athletes look past the color of someone's skin. I have never understood how one man could hate another man just because his skin color is different. It seems absurd to me. We have come a long way, but we still have a long way to go.

# National Champs

There was no indication that the 1988 football season was going to be special for us at Furman. In fact, we were picked to finish seventh in the Southern Conference in some pre-season poll. I always thought that a pre-season poll was a bunch of hype anyway. A pre-season poll is about like someone reading your palm. People pay money to have someone tell them what is going to happen in the future, but most often the information given turns out to be wrong. Isn't that a waste of money?

In 1988, our team went 13 – 2. The only losses were to Clemson and Marshall. Clemson was supposed to beat us because they were an ACC powerhouse led by Coach Danny Ford. We lost to Marshall in the regular season at their place, but turned around and beat them at their place in the playoffs when it counted. We not only won the Southern Conference championship that year, but we also won the I-AA National Championship against Georgia Southern in Pocatelo, Idaho.

All indications were that Georgia Southern would beat us in the national championship game, but we believed. That was all that really mattered. We have all witnessed major upsets in sporting events. The 1988 season was a prime example of some major upsets. We had a great system at

Furman, and our players believed because our coaches had a great plan. Our coaches always came up with a plan that would give us a chance at victory. There is a fine line between winning and losing, and once you get on a winning streak, you become very hard to beat. Every time we stepped onto a field, we expected to win, and we did.

Being the best at whatever you do should be your top goal. No one should strive for being number two. Second place is nice for some I guess, but not for me. To me, second place is the first loser. That may seem harsh, but not to me. I want to win all the time. I want to play fair, but I want to win. There is no need for me to apologize for being a fierce competitor. True champions are always prepared for the finals. True champions do not have to get ready for a championship. They are always ready for the championship. It is ok to dream of being a champion, but you have to work your plan in order to make that dream a reality.

Once a man wins a championship, he wants to win another and another and another. That 1988 football team at Furman put a taste for championships in my mouth. That desire has never gone away. Championships are very hard to come by, so when you get one, you need to be able to enjoy and appreciate your accomplishment.

You can take the above paragraphs and apply it to your business and personal life as well. If you are in sales, be the best. If you are a lawyer, be the best. If you are an Educator, be the best. If you are a doctor, be the best, and I will be your patient. If you are married, strive to be the best spouse that you can be. Whatever you do, strive to be the best.

Anything in life that is worth having does not come easy. Winning championships, having a successful relationship, and being the best in your profession takes a lot of sacrifice. Some people may not be willing to do what it takes to be the best. Don't settle. Always strive for perfection, but know that perfection can never be achieved. Always work to be the best. Always give your greatest effort. At the end of the day, you will be able to know that you did all that you could do. Never put yourself in a position of saying "What if I had given just a little more effort?"

# President George Bush

When you win the national championship, a lot of nice things occur. The city of Greenville threw us a ticker tape parade. It was an amazing experience. People were hanging out of high rise buildings, and dancing in the streets. It was a major party. Everyone was so excited that we ended up having three National Championship Football Banquets. The second banquet had Coach Sam Wyche as the key note speaker. Coach Wyche had played football at Furman, and he was currently the head football coach of the Cincinnati Bengals. The Bengals had just played in the Superbowl against Joe Montanna and the San Francisco 49ers.

The greatest moment of the championship celebration came in February of 1989. President George Bush had just been elected as the President of the United States, and he was making a tour to several states to thank the people for their support during the election. The state of South Carolina played a vital role in getting him elected, and he was scheduled to be at the state capitol to address the state lawmakers. Several of the Furman officials arranged a photo shoot for our team with President Bush. That was a major thrill for all of the guys on the team. There are not very many people that get the chance to meet the President after winning a championship. I was lucky enough to be one of those people.

I was never the greatest player. In fact, I was merely a walk-on student-athlete. I was a member of the scout team for three years before I ever got to dress out for one of the games at Furman. In fact, I never played very much in a game. That was never my goal. There were players that were a lot more talented than me athletically, but I was there to prepare myself to coach.

# Greer High School

While I was a student at Furman, I majored in Health and Exercise Science. I knew that I wanted to coach, and getting certified as a teacher was a top priority. It was crucial for me that I begin my career in a school with a winning tradition in football. My plan was to request such a school for my student teaching. My thought process was to do a great job as a student teacher and volunteer as a football coach. My plan worked like a charm, and I was assigned to student teach at Greer High School. Greer High was the best place to break into coaching. The football team was the best in the county, and usually made a run in the state play offs. The team had actually won the state championship the year before I started student teaching. That team had a perfect record of 15 − 0. It was the first time that a football team had won fifteen games in a single season in the state of South Carolina. I was in the right place.

I was assigned to teach several physical education classes. This put me right in front of the head football coach every day. His name was Stuart Holcombe, and he gave me a chance as a junior varsity football coach. He also let me scout opponents on Friday nights. I took the opportunity and ran with it. I did the very best that I could, hoping that Coach Holcombe would want to hire me when my student teaching ended. It worked.

I was hired as a full time teacher and coach at Greer High School when I finished my student teaching. I ended up staying at Greer for the next five years. Every year, Coach Holcombe promoted me and gave me more responsibilities. I started as an assistant junior varsity football coach, and ended up being an assistant varsity coach on a team that once again went undefeated with a (15-0) record and a State Championship.

# Goals

O ne day I was sitting at my desk and Stuart Holcombe walked in with a video tape. He told me to watch the tape and study it. I figured that the tape was of an opponent, but it was something different. It was a motivational tape geared for businesses. It was the "Do Right" tape by Coach Lou Holtz. He was the head football coach at The University of Notre Dame at the time. Coach Holtz talked about how he had written down a lot of goals, and set out to achieve them. It made a lot of sense to me. I decided that I would write all of my goals down.

These were not just professional goals. These goals included personal things that I wanted to do. I began writing them down, and did not stop until I had about 115 things that I wanted to do. I wanted to read the Bible all the way through. I did that twice. I wanted to learn how to fly an airplane. I did that. I wanted to be on national television, and I have done that a lot. I wanted to meet the President of the United States, and I have met four of them. One of them actually landed on my football field in Marine – 1. I wanted to be a head football coach of a Division – I School. I did that. I wanted to write a book, and decided to write one page a day until it was completed.

I wanted to run for, and become the President of the United States. I am running now. If the people see it my way, I will become the 47th President.

There are also some goals that I wrote down that I am still waiting to accomplish. I would like to sit with world leaders and discuss how we can make our world a better place. I want to have dinner in the White House before I become the President. I want to be interviewed by Oprah Winfrey. I want to be interviewed by Steve Harvey. I want to be on the "Tonight Show." I want to be interviewed by Don Lemon. I want to be interviewed by Rachel Maddow. I want to be interviewed by Anderson Cooper. I want to be interviewed by Yolanda Adams. I love all kinds of music, and I would like to play the piano for Motley Crue when they perform the song "Home Sweet Home." Since I love many genres of music, I would like for the following artists to be on stage singing the song with Motley Crue while I am playing the piano: Yolanda Adams (Gospel), Jennifer Hudson (R & B), Kenny Chesney (Country), Pitbul (Hip Hop), and Bruno Mars (Pop Rock). I have always prided myself with bringing people together from all walks of life, and I believe that bringing all of these artists together would literally bring the world together for a moment in time.

These are goals that I am striving for every day. I intend to accomplish all of my goals. I am definitely having a great time working towards all of them.

In order to make progress in your life, you have to know what you want out of it. My goal list is just that. It is mine. It is not good enough just to write down your goals. Once you have written them down, you have to put a plan into action to achieve your goals. Then, get busy working on your goals. It is never too early and it is never too late to start working on the goals you have set for yourself.

Sometimes it is easy to get lost, especially when you are taking a vacation. A lot of times you will continue to drive around in circles because you are too proud to stop and ask for directions. Some people would rather stay lost for several hours, and drive aimlessly instead of just stopping and asking for help. The same thing happens when you do not have a plan for your life. Write your goals down on paper. Goals give you direction, and keep you focused on your future accomplishments.

# State Champs

I t was 1994, and I was entering my fifth year at Greer High School as an Educator and football coach. I had enjoyed a lot of success as a young high school football coach, and once again, our team was expected to be really good. The team was made up of mainly juniors and seniors. Two years earlier, I was the head junior varsity football coach, and we had gone undefeated. Those same players were now juniors and seniors. They knew how to win, and knew what it took to win. Winning does not just happen. It takes a lot of work. It takes talent, and it takes a little luck at times.

We began summer camp knowing that we were going to be state champs. We were not over confident. We were just sure of our abilities. We averaged 36 points on offense, and we had nine shutouts through out our 15 – 0 campaign. Just like any championship team, we had great players, great coaching, and a little luck along the way.

Everyone wants to win a championship and be in the spotlight. To get to the championship, you have to be willing to make sacrifices. You have to be willing to put the team ahead of yourself. You have to be willing to work harder than everyone else.

That season was great, and I will never forget it. Winning is fun. It does not matter what level you are coaching or playing on when you are winning. I would much rather win at a small school instead of losing all the time at a Division – I school.

Even though we went 15 – 0 and won the state championship in 1994, we had some tough times that we had to go through as a team. We had breezed through the regular season and first round of the playoffs. Things quickly changed during the second round of the playoffs. We were playing Seneca at home, and they were also a perennial powerhouse. We came out flat, and were trailing 13 – 0 at the half. During halftime, Stuart Holcombe had every player and coach on the team get in a big circle in the field house. Then he told all of us to grab hands. He looked at us and said: "I don't know who it is going to be, but someone is going to make a play at the beginning of the third quarter, and it is going to set us on fire. We are going to win this game together."

We kicked off to Seneca, and stopped them three plays in a row deep in their own territory. On fourth down, they lined up to punt. It seemed like any normal play, but not to Knox White. He was one of our defensive ends, and he broke free towards the punter. He blocked the punt, and fell on it in the end zone for a touchdown. All of a sudden it was a new game. He was the guy that stepped up. He was the guy that Coach Holcombe was talking about during his half time talk. Later in the third quarter, Justin Hill, our quarterback, hit Derrick Bruton on a 53 yard pass for another touchdown. We made the extra point and took the lead 14 – 13. There was no score on either side for the rest of the game. We had won, and advanced to the third round of the state playoffs because we believed.

The very next day, one of our assistant coaches, Joel Rice decided to take his wife to see the movie "Forest Gump." Coach Rice and his wife never made it to the movie. A drunk driver hit them, and Mrs. Rice was killed in the accident. We had just been on the highest of highs less than 24 hours earlier by beating Seneca. Now we were on the lowest of lows. It was a tough week, but champions find a way to overcome adversity. Our team attended the funeral, and continued to prepare for our next opponent, Dutch Fork. It was a sad week, but we came together, and beat Dutch Fork thrusting us into the Upper State Championship game against Clinton High School.

We had to go on the road to play them, and it was truly a hostile environment. We played in front of nearly 18,000 people that night, and our defense and kicking teams rose to the challenge. We won 22 – 0, and were headed to the state championship. I have always believed that you must play great defense, and be solid in the kicking game in order to win on the road. We did just that against Clinton.

The championship week was truly special. We had pep rallies every day, bon fires every night, media at every practice, and most of all Coach Rice was back with the team. He was confined to a wheel chair with a broken leg, but he was there. We had a great week of practice, and we were getting ready for the Lower State Champions, the Manning High Monarchs. We would play in Columbia, South Carolina at Williams – Brice Stadium, the home of the Gamecocks. They were a powerful football team lead by Coach Andy Heady. He was a hard nosed Vietnam Veteran. His players were hard nosed just like him. It was a great game, but we came out victorious by a score of 22 – 7. We were champs! We were the best in the state! It was a great experience that we would never forget.

# C.E. Murray High School

A fter the 1994 season, several schools wanted to talk to me about being their head football coach. I went through the interview process for three different schools, and was a finalist for all three jobs. I did not get offered any of the three jobs. The third school that I interviewed for was the team we had just beaten for the state championship. I was really interested in the Manning job, and it looked as if I was going to be their coach, but at the last minute, their athletic director went in a different direction. I was heart broken. The question entered my mind, "Will I ever get a chance to be a head football coach?" Things changed very quickly.

Two days later, I got a call from a coaching buddy that asked if I would be interested in the head coaching position at C. E. Murray High School. The school was in the lower part of the state in Williamsburg County. The school was in the middle of the country, and most of the students came from homes with little to no income at all. The school facility was in bad shape, and most of the students had to ride the bus because they lived in poverty. The football team had only had one winning season, and they did not have a true stadium. There were only about 300 students, and that included seventh and eighth graders. Was I interested? Of course I was interested. I wanted to be a head coach. It was an opportunity.

I took the job, and people thought I was crazy. Why would I leave Greer High School? Greer was rich with tradition, and a great school. Greer had just won the state title, and was expected to be great again. People thought that I had lost my mind. That was fine with me, because I had an opportunity to prove myself as a head coach. I took the position two weeks before August practice began. I will never forget my first practice. We had thirteen players show up. I began to ask myself, "What have you gotten yourself into Robby?" As time went by, more players began to show up. Most of them had been working in the tobacco fields earning money for their school clothes.

C. E. Murray High School was 99% African – American. All of our players were black. All of the assistant coaches were black. I was the only white guy on the team, and I was the head coach. I had no idea that this school was preparing me for coaching positions at several Historically Black Colleges and Universities (HBCU's). We brought the spread offense to the small schools in the lower state of South Carolina.

That first season was amazing. After our first four games, we were 3 – 1. Those three wins included victories over 3-A powerhouse Kingstree, and 2-A powerhouse Saint Stephen. Saint Stephen was led by a guy named Lance Legree that went on to play defensive tackle for the University Of Notre Dame. It was truly a miracle when you compared our team to the other teams on paper. We were way undersized, and way outmanned, but we had a plan, and we worked our plan. We finished that season in the top ten of Class A football and in the state playoffs.

In our second season, we once again had a winning season, ranked in the top ten, and in the state playoffs. C. E. Murray was one of the smallest schools in the state of South Carolina. My father always told me that it does not matter where you are. If you are good enough, they will find you. I guess that is true, because I went from C. E. Murray High School, the smallest school in the state, to the University of South Carolina, the largest school in the state.

# President Clinton

t was June of 1996, and I had just finished my first school year at C. E. Murray High School. I was not just the head football coach. I was also the strength coach. Our weight room was in a trailer on the edge of our football field, and I was straightening up the weights when I heard a helicopter in very close range. It sounded like the chopper was going to land on the roof of my weight room. I went outside and sure enough there was a helicopter hovering over my fifty yard line. The chopper landed, and two men in dark suits emerged and started walking towards me. One of the men asked me who was in charge. I looked at him and said, "I guess I am. I am the head football coach, and you just landed on my field."

The man went on to explain that President Clinton had heard about one of our local churches being rebuilt from a fire. (During this time, a lot of Black Churches were burned in the South.) The church was having a dedication ceremony and President Clinton wanted to attend. C. E. Murray High School was in a very small community called Greeleyville, and there was not an airport in close proximity. The man wanted to know if it would be acceptable to land President Clinton on the football field. I saw this as a great opportunity, and agreed. Over the next 24 hours, work crews removed our bleachers, light poles, goal posts, and a cinder block press box.

The next day, three helicopters landed on our field. The first had Attorney General, Janet Reno on it. The second had the Reverend Jesse Jackson, and the third to land was Marine -1 with President Bill Clinton. I am probably the only head football coach to have the President of the United States land in his back yard.

After the President flew back out, a work crew showed up at our school, and built us a new stadium. It is one of the nicest stadiums in single "A" football in South Carolina. I guess that whatever the government tears up, they must rebuild. It worked out great for C. E. Murray High School.

# USC

I t was the end of the 1996 football season, and Johnsonville High School was playing Lewisville High School for the class "A" state championship. Johnsonville was one of our conference rivals, and their head coach, Doug Hinson, and I had become friends. He had invited me up to see the state title game that was being played at Richburg, South Carolina. We had lost in the second round of the playoffs, and I wanted to wish my friend well, so I went to the game. It was not a close game. Lewisville destroyed Johnsonville that night. There was one player on Lewisville's team that did it all. He played quarterback, running back, defensive back, punter, and kick returner. He scored three times during that game. He was the difference maker. His name was Sheldon Brown.

The next day, I went to Columbia, South Carolina to watch the AAA and the AAAA state championship games at Williams – Brice stadium. One of my former college teammates, Zak Willis, was a graduate assistant coach at the University of South Carolina. Zak was a true country boy. He grew up in the small town of McCall, South Carolina. When I got to the stadium, Zak invited me to sit in a VIP box to watch the games. The entire USC football coaching staff was in that VIP box. I was the only high school coach in the box.

During the first game, Clyde Wrenn, who was the Director of High School Relations at USC, came and sat down next to me. He had been the recruiting coordinator for Clemson when Danny Ford was the coach. During his time at Clemson, they had won the national championship in 1981 by going undefeated and beating Nebraska in the Orange Bowl. He asked me if I had seen any talent at the "A" level that could play in the SEC. I looked back at him and said, "As a matter of fact, I saw a young man last night in the class 'A' state championship game. He did it all. He played a lot of different positions. He was the difference in the game. He is at Lewisville High School, and his name is Sheldon Brown." Coach Wrenn and I continued to talk about coaching, and he thanked me for the information.

I received a phone call three days later from Coach Wrenn. He told me that they had checked out Sheldon Brown, and liked him a lot. They liked him so much that they offered him a full scholarship, and that he had verbally committed to play for USC. Coach Wrenn's next statement threw me off balance. "Robby, it is obvious that you have an eye for talent. How would you like to coach college football here at USC?"

Was he serious? Could this be real? I had sent literally hundreds of resumes to colleges across the country trying to break into college football. I took a deep breath and said "Sure! I would love to have that opportunity."

Coach Wrenn went on to tell me that there was an opening on the staff, and that he was going to the head coach at USC, Brad Scott, on my behalf. I received a call two days later from Coach Wrenn. He said that I needed to drop everything, pack a suit, and get to Columbia as soon as possible.

When I arrived in Columbia, I was treated like royalty. They put me up in a nice hotel, and told me to wait there for further instructions. I waited for almost 24 hours when my phone started to ring around 6:30 pm. It was Coach Wrenn. "Robby, put on your suit, and go to the football office at Williams – Brice Stadium. Get on the elevator, and go to the second floor. The secretary will give you a ticket for the football banquet tonight. You need to hurry." With that, the phone clicked and Coach Wrenn had hung up.

When I got to the football office, I went up to the elevator and pushed the up button. When the door opened, there was Brad Scott, His wife Daryl, and their youngest son, John. We rode up together, and they were very friendly to me. Before we got off the elevator, Coach Scott had already hired me. All I could think was "Wow!" It was truly a mountain top experience.

Just four years earlier, I had been to Williams – Brice Stadium to watch USC play the University of Alabama. During halftime, I went to get a drink with a friend of mine. As we walked down the ramp on the northwest side of the stadium, I turned to my buddy and told him that I would coach here one day. He just laughed at me, and said "In your dreams." Well, I guess dreams do come true.

Sheldon Brown had a great career at USC, and I actually got the opportunity to coach him some. He recently finished his NFL career with the Cleveland Browns.

I spent four years at USC as a graduate assistant football coach. It was a great way for a young single guy to break into college coaching. I actually lived in the stadium while I coached at USC. The hours were long and hard, but the rewards were great. I did not go immediately to the field as a coach when I arrived at USC. The first year was spent analyzing opponent video. Once again, people thought that I was crazy to leave a head coaching position to be a graduate assistant at USC. It was not crazy to me. It was a risk, but it was a calculated risk.

I have always believed that a person's comfort zone is changing in size. It is either getting larger, or it is getting smaller. Taking the position at USC made me step outside of my comfort zone, and ultimately make that comfort zone a lot larger. This can be applied to anything. You can become stagnant if you are not willing to make changes at times. Don't change just for the sake of changing. Change because you know what result you would like to achieve. Then set out to make those changes.

I knew that my first year at USC would set the foundation for my college coaching career. Even though I was not a position coach that first year, Coach Scott let me sit in on every staff meeting. If the meeting started at 8:30, I would be there at 8:20. I was always the first to get there, and the last to leave. Every day was a coaching clinic for me. It was very common to work 18 to 20 hours a day. People may think that is extreme, but in reality it is not. It is sacrifice.

There is an old saying: "Anything in life that is worth having does not come easy." It takes a lot of hard work to be a successful college football coach. It takes a lot of hard work to be successful at anything. If you truly want to be successful in your career, marriage, relationships, or whatever, then you have to be willing to work hard at it.

My first year at USC was 1997, and the team was average at best. We had some great players, but they were young. We only won five games that year because of youth and because of some key injuries. It was a tough year for me because I was not on the field coaching. I was confined to a video camera at the top of the stadium during the game. Shortly after the 1997 season, things began to change.

Coach Scott called me to his office in February of 1998, and said he was making some changes to his staff. He wanted to know if I would be interested in coaching the safeties. Those 20 hour work days had paid off. I had wanted to coach college football since I was twelve years old. It was finally happening. I accepted the new position, and began preparing for the 1998 season.

# Hero

It was Father's Day of 1998, and I had gone to my parent's lake house for the weekend. Our family has always been close, and we always try to get together on holidays and birthdays. I took the boat out that afternoon on Lake Marion. I was by myself, and just trying to relax before going back to work later that evening. The boat trip was just like any other trip that I had made. It was a beautiful day, and a lot of people were on the water.

I came up on a swimming area on the Summerton, South Carolina side of the lake. A lady was screaming, "Help! Help! We can't find her!" About that time, a man pulled a lifeless body out of the water. I ran my boat onto the shore, and rushed to the scene. People were screaming and panicking. A large crowd had gathered around the victim, but nothing was getting done.

I yelled out, "I know CPR!" The crowd parted, and I had a straight shot to the unconscious lady. When I reached her, she was as blue as the sky. She was not breathing. She was gone. Something had to be done. As a coach, you are given a task, and you do it to the best of your ability. My task now was to do whatever I could to save this lady.

I began Rescue Breathing on the lady. It was completely different from training with the CPR dummies. It was real. I had learned CPR when I was a college student. I had worked as a lifeguard at Camp McCall every summer during my time at Furman. After a few minutes, she began to breathe again. It wasn't until then, that I realized that someone had laid her on a USC Gamecock blanket. I stayed with her until the game wardens arrived. Once the game wardens were on the scene, I went back to the boat, and went back to my parent's home. That is when it started to sink in. I did not get frightened while I was helping the lady. I got frightened afterwards. It was real life. I never found out the name of the lady. It did not matter what her name was. She was a human being, and she needed help. That was good enough for me.

The media got wind of the story, and labeled me a hero. Wouldn't most people have done the same thing? I just wanted to be a college football coach.

# 1 - 10

The 1998 season finally arrived, and I was excited because I was finally getting my chance to coach the safeties at USC. I had some great athletes to work with. Arturo Freeman was a pre-season All-American for Playboy Magazine, and played several years for the Miami Dolphins. Ray Green was also a great player that was drafted by the Carolina Panthers. Homer Torrence was a big hitter that ended up signing a free agent contract with the Pittsburgh Steelers. These were the three guys that I had to work with.

We started the season with a 24 – 10 win over Ball State. We were expected to blow them out, but our team was still very young. We were happy for the win, but our youth was evident. What happened next was one of the hardest times of my professional career. We lost the next ten games, and finished the season with a 1 – 10 record. It was a tough time. The Gamecock fans were the most loyal fans that I have ever seen. They packed the stadium every week, even though we were getting drubbed.

The obvious was right around the corner. We knew that Coach Scott was probably going to be fired at the end of the season. When a head coach gets fired in college, usually his entire staff gets fired also. Sure enough, Coach Scott was fired the Monday after our last game against Clemson. I received a complete education on how to bow out with dignity when Coach Scott was fired. He never pointed a finger at anyone, but himself. He took all of the blame.

Coach Scott was fired that morning, and later that afternoon, the athletic director, Mike McGee, wanted to meet with Coach Wrenn, Zak Willis, and myself. He told us that he needed us to continue the football program until he had a new staff in place. This meant that we would have to go on the road and recruit. Over the next three weeks, I spent every day in airports going to see our top recruits. I was recruiting Florida, Georgia, Alabama, Mississippi, Louisiana, and Tennessee. We were holding the recruiting efforts together, and waiting to see who our next head coach would be.

# Lou Holtz

I was recruiting the Mississippi Junior College All Star football game in Corynth, Mississippi, when I got a call from Coach Wrenn. He said I needed to get back to Columbia because an announcement was going to be made that afternoon. Lou Holtz was taking the head coaching position after spending two seasons in retirement from coaching. I caught the next flight back home, and made it just in time to see Coach Holtz accept the position as head football coach at USC. The ceremony was held in Williams – Brice Stadium, and about four thousand fans showed up for the ceremony. Right after the ceremony, Coach Holtz met with the support staff. It was amazing to watch as this man captured the attention of everyone in the room.

Several years earlier, I had watched his "Do Right" video when I was coaching at Greer High School. The video inspired me to the point where I had written out all of my goals. One of my goals was to meet Lou Holtz, and another goal was to work for Lou Holtz. When I wrote the goals down, Coach Holtz was the head coach at the University Of Notre Dame. I actually sent him a letter expressing interest in being a graduate assistant coach at Notre Dame. I received a very nice letter from him turning me down. Now here we were several years later, and those goals were coming true because Coach Holtz was coming to USC.

Coach Holtz only kept a handful of people from the previous staff. He only kept three coaches from the former staff, and I was one of them. I continued to work with the safeties in the 1999 season, and was getting a once in a lifetime opportunity. I had become friends with Coach Holtz's secretary, Rita Ricard.

She had been the secretary for the two previous head coaches, and I told her that if coach Holtz needed anything, that I would be willing to help. She always called me when Coach needed someone to travel with him. I had the chance to travel all over the state with Coach Holtz, and I picked his brain every time I had a chance.

Coach Holtz had to speak at the Gamecock club in Greenwood, South Carolina, and he asked me to drive him there. It was about a two hour drive, and for the first hour he signed autographs for all the fans. Once he finished signing the autographs, he pulled out a manila folder that he had written on. He began to read some notes to me about what it takes to be a successful football coach. I wish I could have taken notes, but I was driving. It dawned on me that he was not reading the thoughts of someone else that had been written in a book. He was reading his own thoughts. How many coaches out there would have loved to have been in that car that day? I am sure that the number is too high to count.

During Coach Holtz's first recruiting season at USC, we had a lot of ground to make up in a short amount of time. Coach Holtz decided that he would fly all over the state in the school plane in order to see as many of the top recruits as he possibly could. In early January, I drove my car to the Sumter Airport to meet Coach Holtz and two other assistants, Buddy Pough and Charlie Strong. When I went in to the office of the small airport, a fellow greeted me and wondered if I was one of the Tennessee football coaches. I told him that I was from USC.

He looked at me and said, "Oh, I thought you were with Tennessee. They are flying in to see some big time recruit, and those two rental cars are waiting on them." I knew that Tennessee was recruiting the same guy we were recruiting, and I also knew that Tennessee had been killing us in our own state in recruiting defensive linemen. I knew that Coach Holtz was due to land a few minutes after the Tennessee coaches, and whoever got to the recruit first would probably sign him. I asked the guy if he could help me stall the Tennessee coaches for a few minutes until Coach Holtz landed. The man agreed. A few minutes later, the Tennessee plane landed, and two of their coaches went into the office to get the keys to the rental cars. The plan worked like a charm, and the man stalled them for about ten minutes. That was long enough for the USC plane to land, and for me to drive right up to the plane. Our coaches jumped in the car, and hurried to the recruit's home, and the Tennessee Coaches were still stuck in the small airport office. We got to the recruit's home first, and we ended up signing Cleveland Pinkney. It was the first defensive lineman that we had beat Tennessee on in years. Cleveland Pinkney had a great career at USC, and went on to play in the NFL for the Tampa Bay Buccaneers.

Coach Holtz's first season, 1999, was very difficult at USC. We did not win a game that year. He was a man on a mission, and I knew that it was only a matter of time before we turned it around. Over the course of the 1998 and 1999 seasons, USC was 1 – 21, losing 21 straight games. It was the longest losing streak in the country. It was painful. It is easy to get up each morning when you are on top of the world and winning. It is much more difficult when you lose 21 in a row. Your food does not taste as good. The days can't go by quick enough. Going through that experience can do one of two things to a football coach. It can make you quit or it can toughen you up. I did not quit. I got very tough. Tough times do not last. Tough people do last.

# Charlie Strong

When Coach Lou Holtz took the job at USC, he had to assemble a great staff to turn the program around. Skip Holtz decided to leave a head coaching position at The University of Connecticut to be the offensive coordinator for his dad. It was a step backwards for Skip, but it got the Holtz family close together, and family is way more important than any professional move. Skip brought two of his offensive assistants from Connecticut, Dave DeGuglielmo (Guge) and Todd Fitch. Dave Roberts had worked for Coach Holtz at the University Of Notre Dame, and he had just left Baylor University. Dave took a position on the staff as the recruiting coordinator. Coach Holtz retained Buddy Pough from the previous staff as his running backs coach.

John Gutekunst (Gutie) had also worked for Coach Holtz as his defensive coordinator when he was the head coach at Minnesota. When Coach Holtz took the Notre Dame job, Gutie stayed at Minnesota as the new head coach. Gutie took a position at USC as the defensive backs coach. Coach Holtz also hired Chris Cosh as his linebacker coach. Cosh had been the defensive coordinator for Nick Saban at Michigan State University, and he had been at the University of Maryland and Syracuse University. Coach

Holtz also retained the two graduate assistant coaches, Zak Willis and me.

My favorite coach that was hired was Charlie Strong. Charlie was hired as the new defensive coordinator. Charlie had been the defensive line coach at Notre Dame, and before that he was the defensive line coach at the University of Florida for Steve Spurrier. Charlie was a player's coach. They loved him. The coaches loved him. The fans loved him. He was and still is a physical specimen for his age. He was in the best shape of any coach I had ever been around. Charlie would run every morning at 6:00 o'clock. I also liked to run, and began running every morning with Charlie. I was nine years younger than Charlie, but age meant nothing when we would run the roads of Columbia in the early morning. I could stay with Charlie for the first two miles, but by the middle of the third mile, Charlie would always pull away. We would usually run four miles, and it did not matter how good I was feeling because Charlie would always pull to the front towards the end of the run. Running was a great stress reliever.

If there was one thing I missed the most when I left USC, it was running with Charlie. He was quite an inspiration for me as a coach. He has a beautiful family. If ever there was a football coach that had his act together, it would be Charlie Strong. Charlie went on to be the Head Football Coach at The University of Louisville, the University of

Texas, and the University of South Florida. Maybe I will get to run with him again, at least for the first two miles.

# The 2000 Season at USC

We had just endured two humiliating seasons at USC going 1-21 with a 21 game losing streak. It was the longest losing streak in the country. It was difficult to endure the 1998 and 1999 seasons, but we dug in as a team, and got stronger during the off season. We knew that we would be better in 2000, but we had no idea how much better we would be. Charlie talked Coach Holtz into changing our defensive scheme. We had run our defense with a four man defensive line, but Charlie had seen a new defense called the 3 – Stack. Joe Lee Dunn had been running this defense at Mississippi State University, and he was having a lot of success with it. One of the assistant coaches at Mississippi State came to USC and taught us the new defense. It was a perfect fit for our team. I had been working with the safeties, but when we went to the 3 – stack, I moved to coaching the Middle Linebackers.

We started the season at home against New Mexico State University. We blew them out, and at the end of the game, thousands of fans stormed the field and tore down the goal posts. We were better than New Mexico State, and we did not have to show our new defense. We played with four defensive linemen the entire game.

We did not show the new defense because we were playing The University of Georgia the next week, and we wanted to catch them off guard. It worked like a charm. The Georgia Bulldogs came to our place heavily favored to destroy us. They were led by Quincy Carter, a Heisman Trophy Hopeful that played quarterback. Georgia was bigger, faster, and stronger at every position, but we outplayed them that day. Quincy Carter threw four interceptions that day. Our defense completely confused him.

One of our defensive linemen, Dennis Quinn, intercepted Quincy Carter twice that day. Dennis was from the state of Georgia, but the Bulldogs did not recruit him. It was amazing. Every time we stopped them, or made a great play, Charlie Strong started laughing. It was true joy with 82,000 fans watching live and a national television audience also tuned in.

We won the game by a score of 24 – 10. Once again thousands of fans stormed the field and tore down the goal posts. The fans marched the goal posts all the way through town, and down to Five Points. Five Points is an area in town where all the college students hung out. The goal posts were cut up into small pieces and sold on line. It was an exciting time. We were 2-0, and Eastern Michigan was coming to us next.

We won that game, and we were 3-0. It was amazing. Just three weeks earlier, we still held the nation's longest losing streak. The next week, Mississippi State University came to Columbia. The Bulldogs had embarrassed us at home two years earlier, and we wanted to have a great showing. It was a close game, and late in the fourth quarter we found ourselves down by six points.

We had the football, and had driven into Mississippi State's territory. On third down, our quarterback, Phil Petty, was hurt throwing an incomplete pass. It was late in the fourth quarter. It was fourth and ten, and our star quarterback was on the bench with a twisted ankle. Coach Holtz took a timeout and told Eric Kimrey to warm up. Eric was the fourth string quarterback. He was a local kid from Columbia that had walked on the football team. He was the son of Bill Kimrey, a local High School Football Coach. Coach Holtz always made the play call in a tight situation, but this was different. Eric Kimrey walked up to Coach Holtz, and said: "I can throw the fade coach!" Coach Holtz looked back at Eric and said, "Yeah, let's throw the fade!"

Eric entered the huddle after the timeout, and acted like he had been there all along. He never appeared to be nervous. On fourth and ten, Eric took the snap, took a quick drop, and threw the fade route up the left sideline to Jermale Kelly. It was a perfectly thrown ball, and Jermale made the catch in the endzone. I have never heard Williams – Brice Stdium any louder than it was at that moment. We kicked the extra point, and took the lead by one. We actually got the ball back with less than a minute to play, and we kicked a field goal. We won the game by four points. We were 4-0.

What are the chances that Eric Kimrey could make that throw coming off the bench? The real question is: What is the chance that Coach Holtz would let a walk - on player make the call? It was a once in a lifetime opportunity. A hero is an ordinary person that performs an extraordinary feat. Eric was the hero that day.

We were riding high and on the verge of one of the greatest turnarounds in college football history. We went to Alabama the next week for our first road game. Phil Petty was still nursing his ankle, and our hero, Eric Kimrey started for us at Bryant – Denny Stadium. It was a very special trip for me because it was at that stadium that I first knew that I wanted to be a football coach. It was twenty years later now. It was a great game, but we came up short, and had to fly home with our first loss of the season. We had our chances, but it was the Crimson Tide's day.

We won the next game on the road against The University of Kentucky. We were 5-1, and on the verge of being bowl eligible. We tried not to get ahead of ourselves, and we took it one game at a time. The following week we were back home against The University of Arkansas. They had embarrassed us the year before in Little Rock. War Memorial is not the largest stadium in the SEC, but it can be one of the loudest because it is bowled in.

It was a new season, and we were one game away from being in the hunt for a post season bowl. There were a lot of emotions during that week of practice. The Razorbacks were coming to us, and it was a pivotal game. Coach Holtz had been the head coach at The University of Arkansas, and he wanted this game really bad. We controlled the entire game, and won. At the end of every winning game, Coach Holtz would address the team in the locker room. He would always present a game ball to a player and to a coach. I was the low man on the totem pole, but Coach Holtz presented me the game ball that day. I could not believe it. It was definitely a defining point in my career to receive the game ball from Coach Holtz on the day that we became bowl eligible by beating his former team. We were 6-1, and Vanderbilt University was next.

We went to Nashville, and destroyed them. Now we were 7-1, and the talk was not just going to a bowl now, but which bowl we would be going to. The Gamecock fans were going crazy. They had been patient for many years waiting for a good team. We were visited by officials from the Sugar Bowl, Orange Bowl, Citrus Bowl, Cotton Bowl, and the Outback Bowl.

The last three games of the season were called "The Orange Crush." We had to play Tennessee, Florida, and Clemson. All three wore orange, and all three had dominated us. We lost all three of them, but we were 7-4 at the end of the regular season. It was one of the greatest turn arounds in Division – I football history.

We accepted a bid to play in the Outback Bowl in Tampa, Florida on New Years Day against Ohio State University. Our fans traveled in large numbers, and that had a lot to do with the Outback Bowl selecting us with a 7-4 record. Also, we were coached by Lou Holtz, a legend. It was a smart business decision for the Outback Bowl.

We began preparing for the Buckeyes. My time as a graduate assistant coach was coming to a close. This was my last season at USC. My last game would be the Outback Bowl. It was a great way to go out, or so I thought.

# Let Go at USC

T he regular season was over, and we were preparing for the Outback Bowl. We were also in the middle of the recruiting season in mid – December. I was in the office breaking down film on Ohio State, when my office phone rang. It was Brad Scott, the former head coach at USC. He was the man that had hired me. When he was fired at USC, he took an assistant coaching position at our in state rival, Clemson. A lot of the Gamecock fans were upset that he had gone to Clemson. I looked at it a little differently. Let me explain. If a CEO of a large bank was relieved of his duties in a hostile takeover, and he was then offered a senior vice president position with a competing bank, then he would be considered to be upstanding for taking the position. He would just be trying to take care of his family. That was basically the same scenario that Brad Scott faced.

Brad called me because he knew that my time as a graduate assistant was coming to a close. He wanted to help me secure a job. He asked me if I had any leads. I told him that I had a couple, but that I was more focused on the upcoming Outback Bowl against Ohio State. Brad was recruiting in Charlotte, North Carolina at the Shrine Bowl. He invited me up, and told me to bring my portfolio. He wanted to get it in the right coach's hands, and he wanted to help me get a full time coaching position. I did not see a problem with it. Coach Scott had actually done the same thing the year before with the other graduate assistant, Zak Willis. I did not hide the fact that I was going to drive to Charlotte to meet Coach Scott. I actually told Coach Wrenn that I was going, and why I was going. One of the other defensive coaches actually helped me put my portfolio together.

I got to Charlotte, and met Coach Scott at the Olive Garden Italian Restaurant. Dinner was great, and we had a great visit. I gave him my portfolio, and headed back to Columbia. The drive only took about an hour and fifteen minutes. I had some more film to break down on Ohio State, and wanted to get back as soon as I could. I was happy to have people helping me find a full time coaching position in college or the NFL. I figured that the more people that were helping me, the better my chances would be of landing a great position. I went back to work, and immersed myself in breaking down film on Ohio State. All was well I thought, but in actuality all was not well.

A week went by, and we were practicing for the big game. We practiced up until December 18th, which was a Saturday. Coach Holtz let everyone go home for Christmas, but gave everyone a time to be back in Columbia. After that practice, we met as a coaching staff to cover some last minute details. At the end of the meeting, Coach Holtz said he needed to see me in his office. In my mind it was no big deal because Coach always had me doing things for him. I was his guy. He was like a grandfather to me.

When I reached his office, I realized that something was bad wrong. He had the athletic director, Mike McGee there also. Apparently someone had seen me having Dinner with Brad Scott in Charlotte after the regular season. The anonymous person had seen me give Brad my portfolio. The observer thought that I was giving up secrets to the enemy, Clemson. How could I be giving secrets to the enemy? We had already played them. I explained to Coach Holtz what had actually happened. I was not released at that point. I was told to go home for Christmas like all the rest of the coaches. Mike McGee did not speak during the entire meeting. It wasn't until I was headed out of Coach Holtz's office that Coach McGee chimed in, "I am shocked!"

I knew then that the situation was not good. A mountain was made out of a mole hill. Looking back, the only thing I did wrong was use poor judgment. South Carolina is a small state, and everyone follows either USC or Clemson. The two schools thrive on controversy. I probably should have declined going to Charlotte, but hey, it is what it is. I was a young coach that was eager to excel in my profession. It cost me dearly.

I went home for Christmas, and received word from a reporter four days later that I had been fired from USC. Could this be real? It was. It made national news. I thought that my career was over. I wanted to crawl under a rock and die. I had done nothing wrong, but I was humiliated, and caught up in the middle of a feud between the Athletic Director at The University of South Carolina, Mike McGee and the former Head Football Coach at the University of South Carolina, Brad Scott. I ended up being the guy that got hurt. I was the pawn. I went from being on top of the world preparing for the Outback Bowl to the deepest valley in what I considered a smear campaign. I actually thought about moving back to my home state of Alabama, giving up football, and working on a farm. I had worked on a farm as a teenager, and thought it might be a great change of pace.

The moment was harsh, and it made me realize that coaching football is a great profession. I had four great years of learning how to run a Division – I football program at The University of South Carolina. I had one bad day. The four years far outweigh the one bad day. You can embrace your career, but there will come a day when your career will not hug you back. You better have a strong support system with your family and close friends. The ones you love will always hug you back.

In order to be a winner, you have to get up when you are knocked down. Successful people find a way to overcome adversity that is placed in their path. I got up fairly quickly, dusted myself off, and drove on. I did not move back to Alabama. I stayed in Columbia, the home of the Gamecocks. I had nothing to be ashamed of, so why should I run from the situation. There was only one way for me to handle the situation, and that was my way. I faced it head on.

# Jimmy Satterfield and Lexington High School

Once the dust started to settle from the controversy I had gone through, I started getting a lot of phone calls from coaches offering me a position on their staff. One call came from a man that had a history with me. It was Coach Jimmy Satterfield. He was my head coach when I played at Furman University. He was a winner. He had retired from coaching for a couple of years, but decided that he still wanted to coach. He had taken the head coaching position at Lexington High School. The town of Lexington is a suburb of Columbia, South Carolina. Could I really take a position on his staff so close to The University of South Carolina? I decided that the only way to handle my adversity was looking straight at it everyday. I took the position as the defensive coordinator at Lexington High School.

A lot of high school coaches stood up for me, but Coach Satterfield carried the most clout. He had graduated from The University of South Carolina. He had won a national championship as a head football coach at Furman University. Coach Satterfield actually let me live at his lake house while I got back on my feet. When I was ready to get my own place, it was Coach Satterfield that made the down payment on my new place. A lot of people say that they are good Christians. Coach Satterfield never wore his faith on his sleeve. He just lived it.

My time at Lexington was a healing process. I was only there for one year, but the people were great. I taught health and physical education, and coached football. At that time, I thought that my college coaching career was over. I bought a condo on the lake, and was happy to be working in a great school.

We had a great player on our team while I was at Lexington. His name was Demetris Summers (Meat). Meat was a star running back that was just a junior. He was the best running back in the state of South Carolina, and by his senior year, he was considered to be the best running back in the nation by most recruiting services. About midway through the 2001 season, Meat broke the state scoring record. Basically from that moment on, every touchdown he scored was a new scoring record for South Carolina high school football.

We made it to the play-offs, but lost in the second round to Spartanburg High School. It was a great season, and I was continuing to heal from my last day at The University of South Carolina. Lexington is a great place. I would have been happy coaching there for twenty years, but my time at Lexington was coming to a close very quickly.

# Buddy Pough and South Carolina State University

We had just finished the 2001 season, at Lexington High School, and several college coaches were coming by the school to recruit some of our players. I was busy teaching health in the classroom, and usually did not get to see any of the college coaches.

Buddy Pough had just been named the head football coach at South Carolina State University. The man before him, Coach Willie Jeffries, had retired, and Buddy was a shoe in for the job. Buddy and I had coached together for four years at USC. He was a high school football coach that had landed the running backs coaching position at the University of South Carolina in 1997. Buddy was in the process of putting together a staff at South Carolina State University while he was recruiting new football players. I had no idea that he was coming to Lexington to recruit one of our offensive linemen.

Later in the day, I saw Coach Satterfield, and he told me that Buddy Pough had come by the school to recruit one of our guys. Coach Satterfield went on to say that he had talked with Buddy about me as well. Coach Satterfield told Buddy that he needed to hire me as his defensive coordinator at South Carolina State. Later that evening I received a call from Buddy. He wanted to talk to me about the position. I had resigned to the fact that I had probably seen my last days as a college football coach. This caught me off guard.

I went to talk with Buddy, and he hired me in February 2002, on national signing day. I had only been at Lexington for one year. I owe a lot of my career to Jimmy Satterfield. He helped me get back on my feet, get a home, and get back into college football.

Anytime there is a coaching change, the team has to get used to the coaches, and the coaches have to get to know the players. The first thing I did was set up individual meetings with every defensive player. I wanted them to know who I was, and I wanted to understand each player that I was going to work with.

We won seven games in 2002 with a bunch of over achievers. We were not very talented in most positions, but we coached the guys hard on fundamentals. One of our biggest wins in 2002 was the game against FAMU. We had to play at their place, but at half time, we were leading 31-0. I believe that our team was just as shocked as their team. It was a great first season, and we set the foundation for several great seasons to come.

The 2003 season was even better. We won eight games, and we were number one in the country in pass defense. Things were great. Winning was and still is fun. It definitely beats the alternative.

By the time the 2004 season rolled around, all of the fans were chanting nine wins. In their minds it was a natural progression. It was not that easy, but we did win nine games, and a share of the MEAC Championship. Once again, we won nine games in 2005. In fact, the two games we lost were by a total of five points. It was our best team in the four years that I was at South Carolina State. We had the seventh best defense in the entire country, and we were fourth in the country in scoring defense. It was an awesome time, and once again, I was on top of the world. It would not last long.

Two weeks after the season, I was in Charleston, South Carolina recruiting when the phone rang. It was the football secretary saying that Buddy wanted to meet with me. I had just gotten a verbal commitment from a great receiver, and was riding on a high. I have always loved the recruiting trail. I drove back to the school, and found Buddy in his office. He looked at me and said, "This is going to be a long day for you."

I looked at him and said "What do you mean?" Buddy looked back at me and said, "I am going in a different direction at defensive coordinator." I stared at him and said, "Wait a minute. I am your defensive coordinator." He looked back at me and said it again: "I am going in a different direction at defensive coordinator."

We had won (18) games in the past two years. I looked back at Buddy and said, "What direction do you want to go in? Do you want to falter?" It made no sense to me. The defense was ranked in the top ten nationally in every major category. One of our toughest opponents, Hampton, was number one in our conference, and they were number one in the nation. Hampton had been averaging over (30) points on offense, and we had held them to fourteen points at their place. Our offense had only managed to score ten points against them. I guess that our defense should have held Hampton to nine points.

It was December 1, 2005, and I was out at South Carolina State University. I got up out of my seat in Buddy's office, shook his hand, walked down to my office, closed the door, and said a prayer. It went something like this: "Lord I thank you for your many blessings. Please give me wisdom in this situation, and let me know what I need to do. Amen." When I opened my eyes, I felt like I needed to go ahead and pack my office. I took the rest of the day to clean my office out. I have always heard that if you stay in the coaching profession long enough, then you are bound to be fired. Usually a football coach gets the axe when he is not successful. It had happened to me twice now, and in both situations, our team was a winner.

# Lost it All

I had spent the last four seasons at South Carolina State University, and we had won a lot of games. In fact, we had won 33 games in those four years. It was a great run. My defensive units had done some great things. We were ranked in the top ten nationally in every major category on defense during that last season.

I had one simple motto for our players. It said, "Eleven Against One." There were eleven guys playing defense, and only one guy on offense that had the football. We were going to gang up on the guy with the football. We never looked at it as being eleven against eleven. I wanted to give our guys a mental edge. If you go into a fight and you are going up against a mob single handedly, your chances are slim. Our players took the mob mentality, and would literally try to punish the one guy that had the ball. It got to the point where the guys would tell each other not to take the ball carrier straight to the ground. "Hold him up so the rest of us can come and get a piece of the action." That may sound cruel, but I don't think so. Football is a Gladiator Sport. It is designed for warriors. It is not meant for the weak at heart.

I was married at the time I lost my job at South Carolina State, and for a while it seemed like my wife was very supportive. We had been one of the best teams in the nation for several years, and I did not think that it would be very difficult to land another job. I was wrong. The job offers did not come, and days turned into weeks, and weeks turned into months. I decided to help a new arena team get started in Augusta, GA while I was looking for my next coaching job. I ended up being named the general manager for the Augusta Spartans, but it was only part time work.

During this time I also decided that I would join the Army National Guard. We were running short of money, and the job opportunities in college football were not presenting themselves to me. I had always encouraged my players in the past to consider the military after college. It was an honorable career, and at worst it would help me with leadership skills. Basic training is hard, but it was even harder for me because I was 38 years old. Most of the guys in my platoon were only 18 years old. I was in great shape, and could run with the best of the best. My basic training was in Fort Sill, OK. It was nick named "Fort Hell" because it gets extremely hot in the summer time. My training was during July and August of 2006, and we went through 17 days where the temperature maxed out over 103 degrees. I lost 30 pounds in nine weeks.

When I returned home from basic training, I found an empty house. My wife had decided that there was no security in my coaching career, and she did not want anything to do with the military life. She decided to move on. All of a sudden, I was without a coaching job. I had lost my family. I had bills to pay, and no idea how I was going to do it. I had a beautiful four bedroom home, with the biggest lot in a nice neighborhood. I had a car payment, a student loan, utilities, credit card bills, and living expenses. I even got real sick for several weeks. I felt like the Old Testament character, Job.

I have always believed that faith that is not tested can not be trusted. Anyone can have faith when things are going great. True faith is determined when a person goes through trials and heartaches. I chose to stay strong in my Christian faith and let God guide me every step of the way. It made absolutely no sense, but I was able to pay all of my bills each month while I continued to look for another coaching job. I eventually sold my home, but it was only by faith that I did not have the bank foreclose on me. Somehow, by the grace of God, I was able to make payments until the home was sold.

I decided that I was going to do whatever it took to get my debt under control. That started by taking a very cheap one bedroom apartment in a bad section of town, and making it my home. From man's eyes, I had lost it all, but I had a plan.

# A Night We Will Never Foget

In April of 2006 during the middle of the wars with Afghanistan and Iraq, I found myself out of college coaching and needing a job. I had always encouraged my football players to consider a career in the military. It is an honorable profession. I decided that I needed to lead by example. So at the old age of 38 when most of the new soldiers were only 18 years old, I volunteered to serve in the Army National Guard.

I was sent to Fort Sill, Oklahoma for my basic training. Fort Sill is referred to as "Fort Hell" because of the extreme hot temperatures during the summer. My training went through the summer months. I don't know where hell is, but it must have been very close because it was hot.

At 38 years old, I was the oldest person in our platoon. There was another soldier in his thirties, but I had him by five years. His name was Doug Frisby. Doug was from Fort Smith, Arkansas. He and I were both the sons of ministers. We became like brothers. I was awarded the position of Squad Leader during our training at Fort Sill. To be a squad leader, you have to be in better condition of those you lead, or you can lose your position by a challenge from any of the trainees.

Even though I was twenty years older than most of the trainees, I could out run them. I had been running five miles a day for many years. Even with a torn hamstring during my time at Fort Sill, I was able to lead the squad and stay out in front. I graduated from Basic Training with honors. It was an amazing experience.

We had been training for several weeks and our platoon was beginning to function like a machine. We had young men from all over the nation and we were truly a representation of the great "Melting Pot" called the United States. Our platoon had young soldiers from Hispanic, Asian, African, and European decent. Everyone was getting along great and working together, or so we thought.

Things were about to change for us. The innocence of these young men and the anticipation of serving our country was about to be tested. As you can only imagine, we had been training extremely hard in heated weather conditions that caused many trainees to pass out during the drills due to heat exhaustion. I will never forget that night in July. Things changed. Reality set in. This was real.

After a long day of training, our platoon had made it back to the barracks. Over the past few days we had been put through the gas chamber, spent a lot of time at the firing range perfecting our marksman skills with our M-16 rifles, and hiked numerous miles with long sleeves, long pants, and a back pack through a heat wave that lasted for 17 days. It was brutal, but we were hanging together creating bonds that would last a lifetime.

That night in the barracks was a defining moment for all of us. The guys had all gotten ready for lights out, but one trainee, Troy Green, had remained in his training uniform. He was pacing around tossing his helmet in his hand. When spoken to, he acted oblivious to anyone else being in the room. I immediately alerted our Drill Sergeant that something was wrong with Troy. Normally when the platoon sleeps, the drill sergeants leave for the night. I specifically told our drill sergent that he needed to stay because Troy was acting out of character. Troy was a good sized young man from Chicago. He stood about 6'2" and weighed around 225 lbs. Back home he had been the toughest guy in his neighborhood. At Fort Sill he was learning that there were guys just as tough or tougher than him.

The drill sergeant did not listen to my warning and left for the night. I had a sinking feeling in my gut that something was bad wrong and so did Doug Frisby. Doug and Robert Garland bunked close to Troy Green so I instructed them to stay on alert and take turns sleeping. I knew that we had a problem, and it was big.

Once the lights went out, our platoon was bedded down for the night. While our young soldiers were trying to sleep, Troy began doing the unthinkable. No one knew that he had a knife. While the lights were out, and our young soldiers were in bed trying to sleep, Troy became a rogue soldier and began stabbing members of our platoon while they were in bed. Seven of our guys were stabbed. Private Roof was actually given a medical discharge because he could no longer serve physically. His lung was punctured. He almost died.

I was ready for something to happen. I had alerted the members of the platoon to also be ready. It happened so fast. We assisted our injured brothers downstairs and out of harms way. There was a lot of blood. It was like a war zone. The rest of the platoon had piled on top of Troy and were going to beat him to death - literally. I yelled "STOP" and they stopped. I then instructed them to hold Troy down until the MP's arrived. I also instructed one of our guys to call for the medics. I told the platoon as they held Troy down that "No one was going to die tonight." We almost lost two of our platoon members that night, but we made it through. No one died, including Troy.

Several people played key roles that evening. It wasn't until the court martial hearing when I had to testify where I realized that I had played a major role in saving the lives of 60 young men. I have done a lot of cool things in my lifetime. I have won championships and spoken to thousands of people, but my greatest accomplishment came that night in Fort Sill.

# Benedict College

I finally made my way back into college football at Benedict College. Benedict, another (HBCU) is a Division – II School. I took the defensive coordinator position and began to put my coaching career back together. I had gone through a year of hurt through my divorce. I had begun to heal, and I felt that it was time to go on with my career.

Benedict College was not an easy situation. They had just started football back, and had a long way to go to be successful on the gridiron. The school is located in downtown Columbia, SC. I was only there for about ten months through the 2007 football season. Our season was not very good. In fact, we only won two games that year. It was the complete opposite of the last season I had coached at South Carolina State University when we went 9-2. Somewhere in the course of that season at Benedict College, I felt like I was going to get my chance to become a head football coach in college. It did not make any sense. Anyone will tell you that college coaches do not get promoted when they have a losing season, but I had faith.

When the Head Football Coaching position opened at Benedict College, I applied for the position and found myself as one of three finalists for the position. On the final interview, the officials of Benedict College brought all three finalists in at the same time. They required all three of us to have lunch together. I found it to be a little odd, but eventually it made sense. The officials at Benedict liked all three of the candidates, and wanted to see if we would be willing to work together. Obviously only one could be named the Head Football Coach, but the officials at Benedict College were in hopes that we could lay our differences to the side, and work together to help the student-athletes succeed on the field and in the classroom. I have always been a bridge builder, and I ended up finding common ground with one of the other finalists. His name was Stan Conner. He had been the Offensive Coordinator at Alabama A & M University. I had been the Defensive Coordinator at South Carolina State University. It seemed like a great fit for the two of us to work together.

Stan Conner ended up winning the Head Coaching position at Benedict College, and he asked me to be his Defensive Coordinator. I needed a job. I liked Stan. He was a good man and still is a good man. I swallowed the pride of not winning the Head Coaching position and took the Defensive Coordinator position. It is amazing how quickly our world can change. I had been the Defensive Coordinator at South Carolina State University, and we were very successful during the four years that I coached there. I had lost that position, lost my family, and hit rock bottom.

I have always been a fighter. This was just another adverse situation that I would have to overcome. The situation at Benedict College was the complete opposite of South Carolina State University. Benedict College had a struggling football program with a limited budget. South Carolina State University enjoyed the rewards of having a much larger budget, great facilities, the full allotment of scholarships, and great student-athletes.

I learned very quickly that we can not dwell on the past. We can learn from our past, but we must live in the present with the expectation of great things to come in the future.

We worked extremely hard as a coaching staff during that 2007 season at Benedict College. The talent pool was very low, but we fought like mighty warriors to help our guys experience victory.

During my one season at Benedict College, I struck up a great friendship with the Running Backs Coach, John Montgomery. He had coached at Texas A&M University with Bob Davie, R.C. Slocum, and Jackie Sherrill. Coach Montgomery had a great football mind, and he had a strong belief in God. He and I became like brothers. John Montgomery was a very loyal coach and loved his family. He had a young son named Mildren Montgomery. John always said that Mildren would grow up to play NCAA Division-I football and go on to play in the NFL. Mildren was just a fifth grade student at the time.

Today Mildren Montgomery is a senior in high school, and he has signed a scholarship letter of intent to play at The University of Tulsa. You see, John Montgomery spoke success into existence for his son Mildren. That taught me a valuable lesson. Whether we speak words of failure or words of affirmation and life upon ourselves and loved ones, those words will come true. I choose to speak words of life and success over my family, friends, and myself.

During that year at Benedict College, I attended church with John Montgomery and his family at Bible Way Church in Columbia, SC. The church was very similar to Benedict College when it came to its ethnic makeup. Bible Way Church, like Benedict College, was mainly African-American. I was the only white person attending the church. It did not bother me. People are people, and I have always looked at the brightness of a man's heart instead of the brightness of his skin.

The dismal 2007 football season was coming to a close, and from the eyes of most people a promotion did not seem to be in order. I was taught as a child that according to I Samuel 16:7 that "Man does not see as God sees. Man looks at the outward appearance, but God looks at the heart." I claimed my promotion before I even received it. I knew it was coming. I did not know how it would happen, but I knew that it would most definitely take place.

The 2007 season ended in late November, and our football team at Benedict College had only won two games. For me to get a promotion seemed to be out of the question. In fact, I told several of my close friends that I felt that I would be a Head Football Coach the next football season. Most thought I was crazy, but I believed.

A month later, on December 22, 2007, my world changed. All of those that thought I was crazy for believing that I would receive a Head Coaching position were left shaking their heads in astonishment.

# Savannah State University

In the middle of December, 2007, I received a phone call from the coaching legend, Willie Jeffries. Coach Jeffries had served as the Head Football Coach at Howard University, South Carolina State University, and Wichita State University. Coach Jeffries was the first African-American Head Football Coach at an NCAA Division-I University. He had coached some great players that went on to have distinguished careers in the National Football League (NFL). He had coached Charlie Brown, who won a Superbowl with the Washington Redskins. He had coached NFL Greats such as Robert Porcher, Robert Geathers, and Jumpy Geathers. Coach Jeffries had retired from coaching at South Carolina State University in 2001, but he continued on at the school as an Assistant Athletic Director. Coach Jeffries was my mentor. I was very fortunate as a football coach to have learned from some great coaches. Willie Jeffries tops that list.

When I received the call from Coach Jeffries, he informed me that the Head Coaching position at Savannah State was open. Coach Jeffries instructed me to drive to Savannah, GA the next day to hand deliver my credentials to the Human Resources Department. I knew this could be a huge break for my career, so the next morning I did as

Coach Jeffries had directed me. I drove to Savannah, GA and personally handed my credentials to the people in the Human Resources Department at Savannah State University. While I was there, I ran into the Vice President of Administration that just happened to be the chairman of the search committee for the next Head Football Coach at Savannah State University.

We all have sent resume's by e-mail, or by United States mail. Only few take the time to hand deliver their credentials. It is a bold move, but it lets the people know several things about you. It lets them know that you are truly interested in the position and want the job. It lets them know that you pay attention to details, but the main thing it tells them is that you are willing to go above and beyond to succeed.

In order for a person to get a job, you have to let the person hiring know that you want the job. Some may call this aggressive. I call it "Leading from the Front." True leaders don't wait for something to be handed to them. True leaders do not make their decisions based solely on opinion polls. True leaders work extremely hard, do what they feel is the right decision, and take it.

If a person helps enough people get what they want in life, that person will ultimately get what they want, but the person must let everyone know exactly what he or she wants. For example, if a person wants a promotion within the company, that person must do a great job, help others on the job, and at the appropriate time let the appropriate people know of their desire for the promotion. If you keep your desires to yourself because of fear, you will ultimately get stuck in a rut. You must keep pressing.

I truly believe that a person's comfort zone is always changing in size. The longer a person stays in one role, the smaller the comfort zone will become. The more a person steps out to view different possibilities in the professional world, the larger the comfort zone will become.

The thrill of success must win out over the fear of failure. You have to ask yourself: "What is the worst thing that could happen if I go for this promotion?" The worst thing that could happen is that you do not get the promotion, but you did gain valuable experience for your next try at a promotion. If it takes a person three attempts on the average to get a promotion, then keep going for it until you get the promotion. There can be "No Fear Here."

After my visit with the Vice President of Administration at Savannah State University, I traveled back home to Columbia, SC. The next day I received a phone call from a member of the search committee for the Head Football Coaching position at Savannah State University. The committee was interested in interviewing me for the position. I was told that approximately ten candidates had been selected to interview from over 150 applications for the position. I gladly accepted the interview.

The first interview went really well. I felt great about it. Savannah State is a Historically Black University (HBCU) and I am not Black. I had just finished a season with Benedict College where we had only won two games. The odds did not look good for me from man's perspective. I was told by friends that it would be a great experience to interview, but that I would never get the job.

The interview went so well that I received a phone call from a member of the committee informing me that I had made it to the final round of interviews. Three candidates had made it to the final round, and I learned later that one of the candidates had been hand selected by the chairman of the committee to be the next Head Football Coach at Savannah State University. That candidate had been informed that he would just have to show up, go through the motions of an interview, and the position would be given to him.

The third candidate had just been fired as the Head Football Coach of another University because of their lack of success. I could not control how the committee voted, but I could control how I conducted myself in the interview.

My interview went well, and I came across very polished with a power point presentation, brochures for each committee member that outlined my strategic plan for making the football program at Savannah State University a winner. The colors of the school are blue and orange. I wore a sharp navy suit, white shirt, and an orange tie. It was subtle, but it let the members of the committee know that I already saw myself as the Head Football Coach at Savannah State University.

The committee met with all three finalists on the same day, and at the end of the day, they had a major problem. Apparently the lead candidate that had been told that the job was his and that the interview was just a formality did not make a good impression. He had come to the interview wearing a green leisure suit with the smell of an alcoholic beverage on his breath. A member of the committee later told me that the chairman of the committee sat at the end of the table with his mouth open in shock during the interview.

The interviews were complete. The committee had to scramble. I had scored higher on the interview than the other two candidates. I had traveled back to my parent's home in Greeleyville, SC for the Christmas holidays, and late that night I received a call from my mentor, Willie Jeffries. He said he had just received a phone call from the chairman of the committee that was also the Vice President of Administration at Savannah State University. Coach Jeffries had been instructed to pick me up, and travel south on I-95 for a late night meeting with the Vice President of Administration at a secret location off the interstate. As Coach Jeffries and I drove south, and the Vice President of Administration drove North, I could not help but think of everything that had led us to this point in time.

We met in Saint George, SC just off I-95 at a McDonalds Restaurant. During this meeting, I was awarded the Head Football Coaching Position at Savannah State University. It had happened. There were only about 225 NCAA Division-I Head Football Coaches in the country. I was one of them now. I was inheriting the worst program in the nation. Statistics will prove that. They had not won any games for a long time. The football program was in shambles. The team only had 22 scholarships compared to other schools that had the full allotment of 63 scholarships. People would think I was crazy to take the job. I thought it would be crazy not to take the job because it presented me with a great opportunity.

Two days later, On December 22, 2007, I was introduced to the school at the half-time of the men's basketball game being held on the campus of Savannah State University at Tiger Arena. A press conference followed where I was introduced to the media. I answered a lot of questions from the media about football, but one reporter from the Savannah News asked me the final question. He asked: "Ok, no one else has mentioned it because maybe they are afraid to touch it, but how does it feel to be the first White Head Football Coach at Savannah State University?"

I looked straight at the reporter, pulled off my new Savannah State Coaching Hat, and said in response to the question: "Am I White?" Everyone in the room broke into laughter. It was a great moment for the school. It was a great moment for me. I never saw myself as the White Football Coach. I saw myself simply as the Football Coach.

The timing of my hiring as the new football coach put us behind in recruiting. I literally went to work as soon as the press conference was over. The first thing I had to do was put a great coaching staff together. Over the years, I had come in contact with some great coaches. Getting the right combination of coaches is a challenge. I received over 200 calls a day from coaches that wanted to come to Savannah State during my first month on the job.

I wanted great coaches that had been in big games, won big games, and expected to get back to big games. At the same time, I was looking for a loyal group of coaches. The task was not going to be easy. In fact, it was going to be difficult. Savannah State had only won five games in the previous five seasons before I arrived. The program was in shambles. I knew that there were some deep problems that needed to be addressed and addressed quickly. I had to surround myself with coaches that would have a singleness of purpose. That purpose was to make the football program at Savannah State into a well respected organization. In order to be well respected, you have to do things the right way all of the time. You have to win in the classroom and on the field.

The first coach I hired was John Montgomery. He came on board as my Offensive Line coach and Assistant Head Coach. John had coached in the Cotton Bowl at Texas

A&M when Jackie Sherrill was the Head Coach. He had coached with Doug Williams, who had a brilliant career as a quarterback in the NFL, and had won a Superbowl as the starting quarterback for the Washington Redskins. John had coached some great players, but I knew that John was a loyal coach. If everything started going south, I knew that John would have my back. At the end of my stay at Savannah State, it was John Montgomery's loyalty that kept me in a positive state.

I hired some great coaches that had won a combined 6 national championships. They knew how to win. It was important that the student-athletes could be coached by men that expected excellence on the field and in the classroom. We inherited a program that had an identity crisis. In order for us to be successful, our coaches would have to lead from the front.

One of my best hires was Alan Hall. I hired him as my Offensive Coordinator and Quarterbacks Coach. He had played quarterback at the University of Miami, and was a part of their National Championship when Dennis Ericson was the Head Coach. Alan had a brilliant mind for football, and he installed a no-huddle, fast paced offense that would gain recognition from around the country. Alan had served as the Offensive Coordinator at Newberry College in 2006 when they won 11 games and made it to the playoffs for the first time in many years.

Once I had assembled the coaching staff, we had to find the best student-athletes for our program. On National

Signing Day, we signed 33 young men that would be expected to contribute very early in their college career.

I remember vividly the very first team meeting that I had. I had just been hired, and the returning players had just returned from Christmas Break. The team had been the joke of the nation for several years. For that first meeting, I addressed the team in a suit. You only have one chance to make a first impression, and I wanted them to know that I meant business. There were 96 young men in that first meeting. As I began to speak, I observed 96 individuals that did not believe they could win. They had lost for many years. In order to be a champion, you must train as a champion, look like a champion, and act like a champion. This group of men was not close to being championship caliber. It was obvious that our coaching staff was going to have to work extra hard to get this team into shape.

As I began to address the team, I raised my hand above my head and told them: "This is the new standard for our program. You are going to have to rise to this standard, or you are going to weed yourself out of this program." I noticed that there was no pride that I could see. You could tell by the way most were dressed, by not being clean shaven, by not having a recent hair cut, and by how they were not acting serious about the direction of the program. As I began to talk to the team about team rules, several got up and left the meeting. They could not handle the discipline that we were about to instill in this team. In fact, out of the 96 that attended that first meeting in January, only 35 made it to the beginning of practice in August. We ended up bringing in 60 new guys that first season. Most were freshmen.

When a CEO takes over a program that has consistently been in the cellar, drastic changes must occur in order for positive results to be achieved. Before I arrived, the players had not been required to attend study hall. They had not been required to attend class. In fact, before I arrived, the starting quarterback had not been required to practice, but would just show up and play the game. After reviewing the problems that we inherited, it became simple to determine the solution. All we basically had to do was the complete opposite of what had been going on before I arrived at Savannah State University.

We required our players to attend study hall, and a coach monitored the study hall every night. We required our players to go to class, and all of our coaches would drop by the classrooms on a consistent basis to make sure the guys were attending class. We required our players to attend practice. If players missed practice, they would not play in the game. My Assistant Head Coach, John Montgomery moved into the dormitory where most of the football players lived. We did this to weed out the problems that we inherited. We required everyone to get a haircut and lose the facial hair. That may seem insignificant, but in the big scheme of our program, it showed that these young men were serious about winning in the classroom and on the field.

We signed several great players that first year, and one of those young men truly stood out. Kurvin Curry was from Hart County High School, and we had a tough battle to win the recruiting war. He was being heavily recruited by East Carolina University as a Wide Receiver. I promised him that if he came to Savannah State, he would be our Quarterback. On National Signing Day, we landed Kurvin Curry. It was a major upset in the recruiting world. This young man was a gifted athlete. I struck up a friendship with Kurvin, and personally made sure that he was always in class. I even worked out with him every day. The success that we enjoyed that first year was because Kurvin Curry was able to lead our team to victory as a true freshman. He was a magician when he had the ball, and an opposing Linebacker's worst nightmare. Our players believed that if Kurvin was in the game, we had a chance to win. As a true freshman, Kurvin Curry broke many of the school records that were held by previous Quarterbacks.

During the 2008 season, which was my first season as the Head Football Coach at Savannah State University, we won as many games as the previous five seasons combined before I arrived. Our team was young, but they believed that we could win. Maybe it was because they were young and didn't know any better. I tend to believe that it was because we had a plan, we did not flinch, and we allowed our players to play and our coaches to coach. People had said that I was crazy to take the job at Savannah State University. Those people were not talking as much at the end of that season.

During that 2008 season, we had to play Winston Salem State University on the road. The experts said Winston Salem was heavily favored to beat us by over 28 points. We won that game by a score of 17-14. Our team fought Winston-Salem every play. With less than a minute to play, Winston Salem had driven the length of the field. Our defense stiffened, and forced Winston-Salem to kick a field goal with five seconds left to tie the game. It was a chip shot. The kicker for Winston-Salem had not missed in the past 20 attempts. He was one of the best kickers in the league. I am sure that the fans watching the game for both teams were thinking that we were headed to overtime. The kick had plenty of distance, but it hit the left upright and bounced straight back. The kick was no good. Our offense took the field for the final play, and Kurvin Curry took a knee to seal the victory. It was only the second time that the football team at Savannah State had beaten an NCAA Division-I team. Our team celebrated like we had won the Superbowl. It was a huge win.

There were several memorable moments during the 2008 season. The team had not won a homecoming game in about seven years. We played Concordia for homecoming in 2008. It was a hard fought game, but we pulled away in the fourth quarter to win the game. When the game was over, a gentleman came up to me with tears in his eyes. He had graduated from Savannah State many years ago. He told me that he had never seen Savannah State win a homecoming game until that day. To me it was just one game. Our team approached every game to reign victorious. To most of the alumni, winning the homecoming game was the only game that mattered to them. It made me realize that winning the homecoming game was very important. I coached at Savannah State for two seasons. We won the homecoming game both years. This kept the alumni very happy.

It was not easy at Savannah State. We had to fight for every win, but that made our victories that much sweeter.

# Discrimination and Lies

The day after I was introduced as the new Head Football Coach at Savannah State University, the Savannah Morning News ran an article about my hiring. In the article, one of the prominent Savannah State fans made a comment that he had to pick his jaw up from the floor. He did not agree with Savannah State hiring a White football coach. He went on to say that there were many capable Black coaches that were available.

I have never read too much into press clippings, but I did take notice of those comments. I wanted to just be the coach. I did not want to be labeled the "White Coach." Because of those comments in that article, many people at Savannah State began to speak their mind about my hiring. All I could control was what I could control. I could not control the thoughts of others. There were several prominent staff members at Savannah State University that did not appreciate me being there. The majority of the staff was very gracious and worked with me, but there were a few that could not get past the color of my skin. It was sad. You see, I had been raised to believe that all men are created equal. It was Dr. Martin Luther King that said he dreamed of a day when a man would not be judged by the color of his skin, but by the content of his character.

After the first season, our team had posted the best record the school had seen in many years. The alumni, fans, student body, and most of the staff were happy with the new direction the team was taking. There was a few on staff that did not want us to succeed. It was the same few that had a problem with my hiring. These few individuals made it very difficult for our staff. These few individuals placed our football program under a microscope looking for anything to bring us down. My every move at a game was scrutinized by this group. I was ridiculed for all sorts of crazy things. I was ridiculed for eating a meal after a game. I was ridiculed for speaking to alumni during warm ups. I was ridiculed for having a coach's show. One of the individuals reported that we had two minor violations to the NCAA. Both of the minor violations included individuals that were White. I was ridiculed because we overspent that first season, and they made me personally repay the amount that was overspent.

This small group of individuals was not going to rest until I was no longer the Head Football Coach at Savannah State University. I have always believed that "Right" will ultimately win out. "Right" ultimately won out in this situation, but it was a difficult battle.

Immediately after my second season at Savannah State University, I met with the Athletic Director, Assistant Athletic Director, and the Vice President of Administration. In that meeting, I was informed that the Athletic Director was leaving to take a similar position at another school. His interim replacement would be the Assistant Athletic Director. She was a part of the small group that did not want me to be the coach at Savannah State. At the end of the meeting, the Vice President of Administration informed me that the President was very happy with my job, and that I had been awarded a one year extension on my contract. The next day I was summoned to the Interim Athletics Director's office. I was told that she received calls all the time from coaches that wanted to be the Head Football Coach at Savannah State University. She also told me that if it were up to her, I would be dismissed.

Approximately two weeks later, I signed that contract extension, and my coaching staff signed as well.

My staff and I were on the road recruiting in January when I received a call from the Interim Athletic Director that I needed to come back to campus for a meeting with her and the Vice President of Administration. To be called off the road from recruiting is never good. I knew that the Interim Athletic Director wanted me to be dismissed.

There were four people at the meeting that included the Interim Athletic Director, the Vice President of Administration, an Administrative Assistant, and me. The meeting did not last very long, but they had put together a list of things they were not happy with. Just three weeks earlier, the Vice President of Administration and the President of Savannah State were happy with the direction of the program. Things changed quickly. In that meeting, the Vice

President of Administration told me that I would never be able to reach the alumni at Savannah State because I was White. He went on to say that I would never be able to reach the people of Savannah, GA because I was White and my fiancé was Black. Was this 2010 or 1960? I could not believe what I was hearing. The alumni were happy with me because we were winning, and we were winning homecoming, which was their main concern.

The Vice President of Administration went on to say that I could resign or be terminated. Either way, I was no longer going to be the Head Football Coach at Savannah State University. All of this occurred a few days before National Signing Day in February 2010. The Vice President of Administration promised that all of the recruits that had been offered scholarships and committed to Savannah State would receive their scholarships. That was true except for five recruits. You see, the five players that did not receive their scholarship were White. Now we had a problem. If it had just been about me, I would have moved on. It was not just about me. These five players were devastated. Their families were hurt and angry.

Two weeks after I was forced to resign at Savannah State, I held a press conference in Atlanta, GA with my legal team. The Interim Athletic Director had called me a couple of days before the press conference to inform me that Savannah State needed a formal resignation letter from me. I was happy to oblige and submitted the resignation letter at the exact time of my press conference. I actually read the resignation letter, which blasted the Administration at Savannah State, during the press conference. In the letter, I gave a detailed account of the meeting where I was forced to resign. Obviously the resignation letter claimed racial discrimination against me and the five recruits that were denied their scholarships.

After in depth consultation with my legal team, we filed suit in Federal Court in Atlanta, GA for wrongful termination due to racial discrimination in the work place. This would be a major fight. I knew that the officials at Savannah State would not admit to the actual events that took place. I also knew that the officials at Savannah State would give untrue explanations for my dismissal. When a person accuses an institution of higher learning of racial discrimination, the school is not going to admit fault. In fact, the school will do everything in its power to destroy the reputation and character of the accuser. This was true in my lawsuit as well as a previous and similar lawsuit by the former Head Baseball Coach against Savannah State University. This coach had the longest winning streak in NCAA Division-I Baseball history, and he was terminated due to racial discrimination. Savannah State officials gave nearly the same explanation for both of our dismissals.

Once my lawsuit was filed, the state of Georgia did a full investigation. For every lie that Savannah State released regarding my dismissal, I showed proof that they were not being truthful. In a sit down interview with the local NBC affiliate, a Savannah State official said that I was insubordinate because I recruited outside of the state of Georgia after I was told to stay within the state to recruit. This individual also said that I was the only football coach that recruited outside of the state of Georgia.

This was completely untruthful by Savannah State University, and I proved it by copies of travel receipts by all of our coaching staff that showed that we all went out of the state of Georgia to recruit. There had never been a directive to only recruit within the state of Georgia.

The same Savannah State official said that all of the student-athletes that were given scholarships were from the state of Georgia, and that was why the five recruits that were white did not receive a scholarship. There were two problems with this statement as well. One of the five recruits was from the state of Georgia. This proved that the Savannah State official was being untruthful. Also, on National Signing Day, an out of state player from Tampa, FL was sent a scholarship from Savannah State University. This student-athlete was Black. Once again it proved that Savannah State was being untruthful.

The show "Outside the Lines" of ESPN and USA Today got information about the story, and sent a crew to interview me, the former baseball coach, and officials at Savannah State University. The show aired in May of 2010, and USA Today ran the story in the summer of 2010.

After the state of Georgia completed their investigation, several people named in the lawsuit were relieved of their duties including the President of Savannah State University, the Vice President of Administration and the Interim Athletic Director. Once the state of Georgia had cleaned house and hired new personnel, their attorneys contacted my legal team. My legal team was informed that personnel changes had been made at Savannah State University regarding everyone named in my lawsuit. They went on to ask my legal team if I would be willing to settle the case.

I agreed to seek a settlement through a Federal Court proceeding. The federal judge ordered Savannah State University to make restitution to me in the form of a financial settlement of $350,000. $110,000 went towards legal fees and court costs. The judge also ordered a joint press conference where Savannah State University had to admit that I did not break any NCAA rules, and that I was the most successful Head Football Coach at Savannah State University in over a decade. I agreed to the settlement. It set precedence in the state of Georgia because no depositions were ever taken in my case. After the state concluded their preliminary investigation, the evidence was overwhelming that I was telling the truth and Savannah State was being untruthful.

On November 21, 2011, a joint press conference was held on campus at Savannah State University in Tiger Arena. It was the same building that I was introduced as the new Head Football Coach just four years prior. Officials at Savannah State welcomed me and my legal team with open arms. During the press conference, both sides wished each other well. It was the end of that chapter of my life. It was the end to that chapter of my career. When you approach the end of one chapter, it is merely the beginning of the next chapter. Expectations of a new chapter and a new direction were on the horizon. It was time. The next chapter would begin in approximately two hours.

# It's Time

Approximately two hours after the joint press conference with Savannah State University where we wished each other well, I held my own press conference at Washington Square in Savannah, GA. The press conference would catch a lot of people off guard, make them scratch their heads, and even make them wonder if I had gone insane. The announcement that I made was not a spur of the moment decision. I had known since I was eight years old that I would make this announcement one day. At the young age of eight years old, I watched my family friend, Jimmy Carter, win the White House. My father had worked with President Carter when he was the Governor of Georgia. My father sat on a committee to oversee the special needs children in the state of Georgia. My older sister was special needs, and it was a great fit for my father to serve on this committee.

I remember the night that President Carter won the election, and how it inspired me. One day I would do it too. President Carter was not considered to be a career politician. He had been a farmer in Southwest Georgia before becoming the Governor of Georgia. I knew from a young age that I did not have to be a lawyer. My preparation began that night as an eight year old child that realized that anything is possible in this country.

The day was here. It was time. It was a new chapter. It was a new direction. It did not matter what anyone thought. I had sought council from my minister, my family and friends, and I had prayed about this decision for many years. On November 21, 2011, I announced at Washington Square in Savannah, GA that I would be running for President of the United States as an Independent. The media had a field day with it. A political Science professor commented on television that I had no chance. There were two major goals that I wanted to accomplish in the 2012 election cycle. President Obama was the incumbent, and realistically it would be impossible to win against him. The two major goals I wanted to accomplish were to 1) get my name out there and 2) gain experience in the debate process. I knew that I would not be allowed to debate President Obama in the primaries, and the Republican field was already full. I chose to run in 2012 as an Independent because I would be able to travel the country and meet thousands of people. This step alone would help me accomplish the goal of getting my name in front of the American people. I needed the debate practice, and in order to gain that experience, I sought the nomination of several small parties in order to get in the debates. My plan worked like a charm. I was allowed to participate in ten Third Party debates.

As a former college football coach, I understand the value of practice. I have never thought that "Practice makes perfect." Anyone can go through the motions of practice.

"Perfect practice makes perfect." An individual must practice as if each moment is that defining moment when all is on the line, and only perfect moves will give you victory. I needed a debate coach, and found a gentleman by the name of Al Pisano to help me prepare for the debates. Behind every great athlete is a great coach. For example, the Dallas Cowboys won Superbowls with several great coaches – Tom Landry, Jimmy Johnson, and Barry Switzer. Michael Jordan and the Chicago Bulls won six NBA Championships with Phil Jackson as their coach. The University of Alabama won numerous National Championships with the great coaches, Paul "Bear" Bryant, Gene Stallings, and Nick Saban. It was just as important for me to have the best debate coach for my 2012 practice round. Al Pisano proved to be a great asset who was able to prepare me for the debates.

When the debates began, I was prepared. I did well in every debate. Ultimately, Virgil Goode won the Constitution Party nomination for President in 2012. Mr. Goode was a former Congressman from Virginia. Believe it or not, the 2012 election cycle was perfect for me. I had accomplished my two goals. I had traveled the country, met thousands of people, and gained valuable experience debating.

When I started my 2012 campaign, it was just God and me. I did not have a huge following, but I knew the principle of hard work paying off. I have always believed that positive activity towards a goal will yield positive results. This can be applied to anything.

One month after I announced that I was running, I decided to get in front of as many people as possible in a short period of time. I decided to campaign during the college bowl season in early January 2012. It was a great fit. I am a former college football coach and the college fans were very receptive. I was able to meet many people from all walks of life. This college bowl tour began in Charlotte, NC at the Belk Bowl. The University of Louisville was playing North Carolina State University. My plan involved getting to the games at least six hours before kickoff, and campaigning in the parking lots while all of the fans were tailgating. Thousands of people from Louisville, Kentucky and Raleigh, North Carolina were all in the same location. I took that time to shake as many hands, pass out campaign cards, and take pictures with thousands of people.

The next bowl, the Chic-fil-A bowl was in Atlanta, Georgia. The University of Virginia was playing Auburn University. Once again, I was able to meet with thousands of fans and students from two states. Where else was I going to be able to get in front of 35,000 people from Virginia and 35,000 people from Alabama in the course of only a few hours? The plan was working. My name was getting out to many people.

I left Atlanta, Georgia and headed to Jacksonville, Florida for the Gator Bowl. Ohio State University was playing the Florida Gators. This gave me an opportunity to meet with thousands of people from the states of Florida and Ohio. I rushed across the state that afternoon to campaign at the Capital One Bowl in Orlando, Florida. The University of South Carolina was playing the University of Nebraska. I met thousands of people. I listened to their concerns about our nation. I gave them my solutions. I realized that all of us want a great America. All of us want to see our country have an economic recovery.

As I met with all of these people from across the nation, I realized that this campaign was truly for them. They had the same concerns and frustrations that I have had for years.

I left Orlando, Florida and traveled down to Miami, Florida for the Orange Bowl. I was able to reach thousands of people from the states of South Carolina and West Virginia because West Virginia University and Clemson University were competing.

I left Miami and drove north to Birmingham, Alabama for the Compass Bowl. Southern Methodist University was playing the University of Pittsburg. This gave me the opportunity to meet folks from Texas and Pennsylvania. Although I was meeting people from all over the country, I kept hearing the same concerns. People wanted the manufacturing jobs brought back, energy independence, better treatment for our military personnel and Veterans, and a chance at the American Dream.

I left Birmingham and traveled down the state of Alabama to Mobile for the Go Daddy.Com Bowl. Northern Illinois was playing against Arkansas State University. This put me in front of thousands of people from the states of Arkansas and Illinois. I left Mobile, Alabama and traveled to New Orleans, Louisiana for the National Championship game between the University of Alabama and Louisiana State University. Bourbon Street was a wild place. Over 750,000 college students and fans were there. I worked hard, met thousands of people, and told them I wanted to be President. I have always believed that you have to tell people what you want in order to get what you want. I also believe that if you help enough people get what they want, you will ultimately get what you want. I want to be the President of the United States.

After the National Championship Game between the University of Alabama and Louisiana State University, I traveled home to Charlotte, North Carolina for a short break. In eleven days, I had been to eight games in five states. The games had people from a total of fourteen states. My name was starting to get out.

When an individual steps out on a limb and does something out of the ordinary, the first thing people do is laugh and think that the individual is crazy. If that individual does not get discouraged and quit, the people will begin to get mad at the individual. "Who does he think he is?" That is a question that most will begin to ask. If the individual continues and does not give up, the people will begin to listen. Then, those same people that laughed and got angry will end up joining the effort of the individual that had the audacity to chase his dream. If that individual will continue to stay the course and keep his eye on the prize, he will wake up one day and will have accomplished the task. I stepped out and stepped up. I will not back down. I will not go away. There are too many people that have hopes in this campaign now.

A few weeks later I traveled to Indianapolis, Indiana for the Superbowl. The New York Giants were playing the New England Patriots. The Superbowl is a very unique sporting event. Unlike most other sporting events, the Superbowl attracts fans from all over the nation. The Superbowl Village in downtown Indianapolis had over one million visitors during the week of the big game. Once again I was able to meet and reach thousands of people from all over the country. The concerns of the people remained constant. I have always asked every person I have come in contact during my campaign this question: "What is the number one issue you would like to see resolved in the United States?" The overwhelming majority of the responses to that question are that people want jobs that will actually take care of their expenses and still have some extra left over at the end of each month. Without economic freedom, an individual actually has no freedom at all.

In 1860, the people of this nation elected an underdog as President of the United States by the name of Abraham Lincoln. The experts did not give him a chance during the election, but he ended up winning the White House.

During his presidency, President Lincoln pushed for the passage of the Thirteenth Amendment, which abolished slavery. I love to study history because it has a tendency of repeating itself. I venture to say that in 2016, it is time for the people to elect a President that has gone through the same struggles as most Americans. In November, 2016 the time will arrive to send a President to Washington, DC that will once and for all push for legislation that will break the chains of economic enslavement that bind every American citizen today. That is what I intend to do.

As I travel across the nation, I have heard many problems from all sorts of individuals. The citizens of this country love the United States and want to see a nation that will once again prosper. The solution, when broken down, is really very simple. I will discuss my plan to restore this nation in the next chapter. Keep reading.

After returning from the Superbowl in Indianapolis, Indiana, I decided to plan a campaign swing that would cover the East Coast and Midwest. This would once again allow me the opportunity to meet thousands of people across the nation, which would help me achieve the goal of becoming a household name across the nation. I set out in March of 2012 from my home of Charlotte, NC, and headed towards the Washington, DC area. That evening I had a dinner meeting with people in Columbus, Maryland. The next day I spoke in Columbus at a small rally. After the rally, I drove to Washington, DC to see my future home. Most may think this is crazy, but I actually went to the White-house, walked the perimeter, and claimed that house to one day be my living quarters as the President of the United States. I do believe that in order to achieve greatness, you have to see yourself in the position way in advance. I have also been taught that as a man speaks, so is he. We as people have the power to speak things into existence. Hard work and preparation must go hand in hand with the speaking, but this principle has proven true on many occasions for me.

I left Washington, DC and traveled to New York where I met with some campaign supporters. After campaigning on Long Island, I met my old friend Chris O'Hare on Staten Island. I had never been to New York City, and Chris took it upon himself to be my tour guide. You have to have some fun on the campaign trail, or you will burn yourself out quickly. It was amazing to walk through Central Park and see Time Square, Madison Square Garden, Ground Zero, The Empire State Building, and Wall Street. That evening we took the ferry by the Statue of Liberty. This statue has represented freedom for millions of immigrants coming to the United States. This country has been built on immigrants that have made the journey to our country in search of Liberty. That must never change. I literally got chills viewing Lady Liberty.

After leaving New York City, I traveled to Buffalo, New York for several campaign stops. Over the course of the first three months to my campaign, I met Liz Abbott. Liz was a student at Buffalo, and I remember the first time she and I communicated. It was on Facebook. I had been posting my campaign material all over Facebook, and Liz had commented on one of my posts by saying "Ron Paul or no one at all." I began to communicate with Liz that ultimately, Ron Paul was not my opponent. It was my desire to prepare myself for the 2016 election. Liz appreciated what I was doing and she said she would like to help. Liz became my Northeast Coordinator for the campaign. Liz Abbott is a jewel to this nation. She loves her country. She is a true Patriot. Liz arranged for me to speak on campus at the University of Buffalo, and she also set up a meeting with the football team at the University of Buffalo where I spoke to the team. Liz found time at the end of my stay in Buffalo to take me to Niagara Falls. It was breath taking.

After leaving Buffalo, I drove through Cleveland, Toledo, and Chicago. The people that I have met came from all walks of life. I have met millionaires and people that are stuck in poverty. There is beauty in every person that I have met on this tremendous journey.

I drove down to Peoria, Illinois where I spoke at a state convention. At the convention, I met a man named Dale Dorch. Dale and I became great friends, and he became my Illinois State Coordinator. Dale has also worked security for me now that the campaign has grown.

After speaking in Peoria, Illinois, I traveled to the Saint Louis, Missouri area where I spent some time with some great people. I went to Jefferson City, Missouri for a huge rally at the State Capital. The rally allowed me the opportunity to meet thousands of people from Missouri. We also found time to actually go up to the top of the Gateway Arch in St. Louis, Missouri. It truly amazed me how great of a structure the arch is. The ingenuity that it took to build the Gateway Arch was amazing. That time in the history of our nation, great pride was taken in building huge things. We need to get back to that.

In April of 2012, the Constitution Party had their national convention in Nashville, TN. By choosing to run as an Independent, I was able to seek the Constitution Party's nomination for President of the United States. Many people within the Constitution Party have been labeled as Christian Zionists and Right Wingers. Even though I am a Christian, I have never had the urge to put a label on myself. I am definitely not a Christian Zionist, and I am not a Right Winger. In fact, I am not way to the Left either. Just like most Americans, I fall somewhere in the middle.

The National Convention of the Constitution Party was held, and the former congressman from Virginia, Virgil Goode, won the nomination. I was happy. Winning the Constitution Party nomination was not my number one goal. My number one goal was, and still is to win the White House as a New Breed Democrat.

# Aaron Lyles

During the spring of 2012 I was traveling across the country and campaigning as an Independent for President of the United States. It was my first run. President Obama was seeking re-election and I knew that he would not have to debate anyone in the primaries. I needed debate experience so I chose to run as an Independent in order to get my name established as a contender, and because I could debate against other candidates that were seeking the nomination of small parties.

The Constitution Party was holding a series of debates and I chose to compete in ten of their debates. Many of the debates were podcasts, but it gave me valuable experience. There were several candidates vying for the nomination. The candidates were John Lewis Mealer of Mesa, Arizona, Susan Ducey of Wichita, Kansas, Dr. Laurie Roth of Elk, Washington, and United States Congressman Virgil Goode of Rocky Mount, Virginia.

It became apparent that Congressman Goode and myself were leading throughout the debates. This set up a showdown in Lansing, Michigan for the final debate.

The debate took place on a Saturday afternoon. My team arrived early and placed campaign signs all over the debate hall. It was a strong tactic for a small party debate.

The other candidates just showed up to debate. I showed up to win. The debate lasted for roughly two hours where it was apparent that I had won this debate over Congressman Goode.

Later that afternoon some of the organizers had a meet and greet for the candidates in a little town called Door, Michigan. One of Congressman Goode's campaign staffers was in attendance. Not only was he a staffer, but he was the nephew to Congressman Goode. They kept their circle very tight. During the meet and greet Aaron Lyles and I sat down and had a fairly lengthy conversation.

Aaron was only twenty years old, but he was a brilliant political strategist. He admitted to me that he entered the debate not liking me very much. The reason was apparent that I was a threat to Congressman Goode, but Aaron said that during the debate, something changed. Aaron said he actually listened to my common sense stance on the issues, and loved how I dealt with the people. Aaron went on to tell me that if I chose to stay in politics, he would like to help my campaign in some capacity because Congressman Goode was going to retire after the election. I accepted Aaron's offer, and we began working together in November of 2012 – just a few days after the election that President Obama won.

I had been gaining support from people all over the country, and Aaron initially was my Southeast Coordinator for the 2016 Rise Up With Robby campaign. It became very clear very quickly that Aaron was in it for the right reason. He wanted to be a part of something that would see our nation prosper like never before. It also became very apparent that Aaron was a political genius. I wanted to make sure that we had the right people in the right positions so I moved Aaron to the position of National Campaign Manager making him the youngest person to ever hold that position for a United States Presidential Candidate.

Aaron and I have been working at this for over ten years now. The Rise Up Movement continues to grow, and we literally have friends all over the United States and all over the world. When you work with someone for that long you become like brothers, and I consider Aaron's family to be my extended family. Aaron and his wife Charlene live in Roanoke, VA and I have made many trips to strategize with Aaron. I made Aaron a promise that I intend on keeping on January 20, 2029. We have got a lot of work to do.

It has been awesome working with Aaron over the past decade. To pay the bills he and I have actually gone into business together a couple of times. The first time was operating a meal delivery service called FoodEx. We had locations in North Carolina and Virginia, and found ourselves profitable from the first day of business as we serviced hundreds of restaurants and clients in the Roanoke Valley area and the University area of Charlotte, North Carolina.

Currently Aaron and I work with Family First Life as Life Insurance Brokers. Protecting families kind of fits with the bigger goal of protecting America. There is never a dull moment.

Aaron and I have seen a lot as we have continued on this political journey. Aaron usually does all the booking for my campaign in Virginia and he coordinates every aspect of my travel and events where I speak.

Aaron has arranged my trips throughout the Midwest, every county in Iowa, the Texas Primaries, the New Hampshire primaries, speaking engagements in Atlanta, Georgia, Los Angeles, California, Miami, Florida, Greenville, South Carolina, Virginia Beach, Virginia, Jacksonville, Florida, Washington, DC, Phoenix, Arizona, Las Vegas, Nevada, Manhattan, New York, Indianapolis, Indiana, and many more places in small town USA. Aaron has also coordinated my speaking engagements in Jinan, China, Mumbai, India, Chennai, India, and Paris, France in the Eiffel Tower. We have done a lot, and for a long time we did a lot with very little resources.

When you step back and start thinking about the noise we have made, especially in the lead up to the 2020 election, Aaron will use the word "Absurd" to describe everything we have been able to do and accomplish with literally little to no resources. Things have begun to change now, and all of it is because we never quit. There is too much to do and too many people to help.

It is a good feeling when you have a business partner that has your back. That is Aaron Lyles.

# 2016- Campaign Trail

On September 22, 2013 I was interviewed on "America's Morning News." This is a national news talk radio show that has over 150 stations nationwide. During the interview, I announced that I would be seeking the Democratic Party's Nomination for the office of President of the United States in 2016. It created some controversy within the ranks of those that are more in line with the Independents and Third Parties. I knew that would be the case, but we needed to give this campaign a legitimate chance at winning the Whitehouse.

In 1992, Ross Perot, a Texas billionaire, ran as an Independent. He had enough money to get on the ballot in every state. Even though he was on every ballot in every state, he was only able to gain 19% of the popular vote and no electoral votes. In order to win, you have to play a game by the rules that are set in place.

Before my announcement, our campaign team looked at the Democratic and Republican Parties. We actually reached out to both parties on a number of occasions. Every time we reached out to the Republican Party, they turned their nose up at me as a candidate. Every time we reached out to the Democratic Party, they welcomed me with open arms. I have always been a bridge builder in my career. I have been able to get people from all walks of life to work together for a common cause. I have taken pride in being able to do that. The Democratic Party does a much better job of reaching out to all people in America. That is very important to me, and it made my decision much easier.

Since I announced that I would be seeking the Democratic Party's Nomination for President of the United States in 2016, tremendous support has been coming to the campaign. In nine months, we have been in 23 states.

I have always thought outside of the box, and I convinced my campaign team that we needed to gain some national television exposure for as affordable a price that we could find. During the spring of 2014 we gained national television exposure by teaming up with NASCAR Driver, Jennifer Jo Cobb. Jennifer is the only female driver in the NASCAR Truck series. Our first race was a huge hit. The #10 "Robby Wells for President" truck debuted in Charlotte, NC on May 16, 2014. Jennifer received over eight minutes of national television time during the race. We also ran the Rise Up Robby Wells for President ARCA car in the spring of 2014 with Joey Gattina as our driver Talladega Speedway. This is called "thinking outside the box."

In June of 2014, our campaign team purchased a tour bus. This bus made stops in 37 states over a five month period. The Rise-Up Tour made stops at fundraisers, rallies, sporting events, colleges, large cities, and small towns.

The naysayers are going to say that I should quit. My thought process has always been this: If I never give up, I am not guaranteed victory, but if I quit, I am guaranteed failure. Is there anyone that wants failure? Of course, no one wants to lose. I will not back down, I will not retreat, I will not surrender, I will not quit, and I most definitely will never go quiet in the night.

Our country was given "Hope and Change" in 2008. In 2012 we moved "Forward" so that in 2016 we can once and for all "Love and Serve" our fellow man. The love of a single mom that is willing to work a job through the middle of the night just to serve her children by putting food on the table. The love of a volunteer that is willing to serve the homeless Veterans without even a pat on the back. The love of an over worked and under paid school teacher that is willing to serve her students so that they will be successful in life. The love of our young people serving in the military by laying their lives on the line every day for you and me. The love of a bald headed football coach that is willing to serve the people as President of the United States, and his belief that this country has a place for him too. The boldness to love and the courage to serve is the future of our nation.

# Eaglenomics

For the past five decades, the people of the United States have elected a President that is either Left Wing or Right Wing in political philosophy. On Inauguration Day the President basically has half of Congress that will fight him on everything that he tries to accomplish. In the past thirty years, we have seen millions of manufacturing jobs leave the United States for foreign soil, constant conflict in the Middle East because we are not Energy Independent, government shutdowns, an educational system that has dwindled every year, and an economic meltdown in the past decade.

I believe that we have come to a point in the history of our nation where we must lay aside our pride and differences. It is time for us to begin working together for a better America. Whether you are Black or White, young or old, male or female, gay or straight, Democrat or Republican, Third Party or Independent, Protestant or Catholic, Mormon or Agnostic, Muslim or Atheist, or those of the Jewish Faith – we are all very unique here in the United States. We can embrace our differences because we have one common bond. We are all Americans. It is time for each of us to overcome our failures due to the fear of each other's unique qualities. It is time to stare down the fear of each other's differences with the face of courage.

The beauty of Eaglenomics is that it takes the absolute best from the Left Wing and the Right Wing. I believe it is time that the people of the United States should elect a President that can see the beauty in both Wings. After all, the President is supposed to represent all of the people. If a bird only has one good wing, flight is not possible. It takes two very strong wings for the bird to soar. I believe that the same holds true for our nation. You see, I am not Left Wing or Right Wing. I am the Bird that sits in the middle. My plan is to pull both Wings to me in order for this Eagle to soar all the way to Washington, DC. As President of the United States, I will be able to meet with a group of Liberal Lawmakers and tell them that this is the most Liberal Agenda they will ever see, but that we are going to use some Conservative tools to get there. I will also be able to meet with a group of Conservative Lawmakers and tell them that this is the most Conservative Agenda they will ever see, but we are going to use some Liberal tools to get there. I will be telling both groups the absolute truth.

Eaglenomics calls for the following:
1. Create prosperity and full employment for all.
2. Develop Sustainable Energy Independence.
3. Reverse International Trade from Deficit to Surplus.

4. Restore and Advance the United States Manufacturing in all sectors.

5. Create millions of manufacturing jobs to improve infrastructure.

6. Fix National Healthcare.

7. Restore Social Security to Financial Health.

8. Enable Financially Sound Local and State Government.

9. Reform both Wall Street and the Financial Sector.

10. Re-Design the Banking System and make it Stable.

11. Structure Educational Support for all Americans.

12. Eradicate the Revenue Deficit and the National Debt.

13. Strengthen the United States Security.

If we continue down the path that we have taken for the last 25 years, the economy will continue to dwindle, our country will continue to stay in constant conflict in the Middle East, our educational system, which ranks 36th worldwide, will continue to falter, and our citizens will continue to be enslaved to our current economic system. As President of the United States, I will be pushing for legislation that will once and for all break the chains of economic enslavement that are binding every American Citizen today. Without economic freedom, we have no freedom at all.

It is time to get Americans back to work. Today we have 20 million Americans that are unemployed and another 25 million Americans that are underemployed. We have nearly 50 million Americans living in poverty, and 149 million Americans that exist on low income. We have lost 4.5 million jobs in the manufacturing industry in the past 15 years due to the massive imports that have resulted from the current trade policy.

It is time to become Energy Independent. As a nation, we must become completely independent on our own energy source. Today, our nation only produces about 35% of our oil supply. The other 65% of the oil that we use comes from foreign countries. Some of the countries we are doing business with harbor terrorists and support terrorist activities. Desert Storm, 9/11, the War in Afghanistan, and the War in Iraq were all directly, or indirectly, caused by America doing business with foreign countries to gain their oil supplies. There are over 9,500 Americans who lost their lives, and multitudes more who have become gravely disabled, in Desert Storm, 9/11, the War in Afghanistan, and the War in Iraq. Our country is rich with natural resources, and as President of the United States, I will push for legislation to become a nation that achieves Sustainable Energy Independence. As President of the United States, I will push for legislation that will allow private companies to help America become an Energy Independent Nation. This will create at least 3 million jobs. This is not only an economic issue, but is also an issue of national security and an environmental issue as well.

It is time to return the liberties and freedom to the people of the United States. With the recent scandals of the NSA, AP, IRS, Benghazi, personal e-mails, and Fast and Furious, the American people deserve a Federal Government that is truly transparent. If our Federal Government is totally transparent, there will be no need for cover-ups, and there will be no scandals. Attitude starts at the top of an organization, and permeates its way throughout the entire organization. As President, I will maintain the stance of transparency. I will also push to return the liberties and freedom back to the people of the United States. As your President, I will work tirelessly to protect every citizen from all enemies, but I will never overstep our Constitutional boundaries. Every citizen deserves privacy, and every citizen deserves the peace of mind that their President will protect them.

The people of the United States deserve a strong National Defense. Before entering office, the President of the United States must take the following oath, "I do solemnly swear that I will faithfully execute the office of President of the United States, and will to the best of my ability, preserve, protect, and defend the Constitution of the United States". The first objective of the President of the United States is to ensure the safety of the American citizens against all enemies. We must maintain a strong military and continue to protect our citizens. My plan is to bring as many troops home as possible.

As President of the United States I will ensure that our military will always be given the resources needed to keep our country safe. We must continue to stay on the cutting edge of technology and remain the most powerful military force in the world.

We must do a better job of taking care of our Veterans. The United States military has always done an incredible job of training our young men and women to protect our nation. We must do a better job of training our troops to become civilians again when their time of service is up. As President of the United States I will push to re-establish the free health care that had been provided for our veterans until recent alterations in policy. As President, I will push to further extend health care for veterans at any private provider or facility in the nation. Our veterans have laid their lives on the line for each and every American, and it is time for Americans to show these heroes our gratitude. Under my administration the veterans are going to receive the love and respect from this country that they deserve.

Currently, we have over 17 million single parents that are raising over 20 million children here in the United States. The system has failed many of these single parents. For example: A single mom is faced with a huge dilemma. If she wants to go to work, her child must be placed in childcare. The average cost of childcare can run from $250-$300 a week per child. That means that the mom is going to have to pay close to $1,200 a month in childcare. If the single mom is working a minimum wage job, this is not feasible. If the single mom has two children needing childcare that would cost her approximately $2,400 a month in childcare costs alone. The current system basically places these single moms in a trap of having to stay at home and go on government assistance. As President of the United States, I will push for universal childcare. Whether the child comes from a single parent family or a dual parent family would be of no consequence. By providing universal childcare, millions of single parents will be given the freedom to go back to work or school. This plan will also create jobs in the childcare industry.

I have always approached minimum wage differently than most. By bringing millions of manufacturing jobs back to the United States, creating millions of jobs to improve our infrastructure, creating millions of jobs in the field of Energy so that our nation can once and for all become Energy Independent, we will create an environment in our country that will take us from having a job deficit to a job surplus. By having more jobs than workers, Supply and Demand will kick in. If there is not enough supply of workers, the demand for those workers will go up. This will force companies to compete for their employees by raising wages and benefits. This is a fairly simple concept that will get our nation producing on a massive scale, and at the same time provide workers with livable wages.

This journey is ongoing, and we have gained a tremendous amount of momentum because our message is clear. It is time for each of us to lay aside our differences. It is time for each of us to begin working together. It is time for each of us to stare down the fear of each other's differences with the face of courage. I love my country.

# Ambassador

When I began the Rise Up movement on November 21, 2011, I was hoping to build a national movement that not only would propel me to the White House, but also inspire others to run for office underneath our umbrella. Sometimes our plans are not big enough because our comprehension is limited only to what we can see, but if we are faithful to God and obedient to His calling in our lives, things can happen that are way beyond our own imagination.

This scenario happened to me about five years into the Rise Up movement. Our team had been working extremely hard to gain supporters in all fifty states, when I received a call that I was needed in Jinan, China. I have always felt at home on stage speaking in front of large crowds. We all have gifts. This is one of mine, but to speak to thousands of people that are from another country - people that did not speak English...this was going to be a challenge.

That first speech on foreign soil in Jinan, China was amazing. As thousands of people filed into the arena, I got to myself backstage, said the Warrior's Prayer, and listened to Tasha Cobbs song "I will Run" on my headsets. As I stepped to the stage, I was not nervous to be speaking in front of more than 30,000 people from China. I was focused and concentrating on the message, making sure that it was on point as I stepped into my purpose. It was an amazing experience. My path was in full motion now. It was time to roll.

When I returned to the United States, I received a phone call from Timothy Roland in Chennai, India. Timothy was the head of the International Human Rights Peace Commission based in Chennai, India. After a few minutes on the phone, Timothy informed me that they wished to appoint me as Ambassador of the International Human Rights Peace Commission and as their International Spokesperson. This was really happening.

Because of this appointment, I have been given the opportunity to speak in front of thousands of people around the world and to millions by international television regarding my plan to achieve Global Sustainable Energy Independence and to improve Education worldwide. This appointment has also given me the opportunity to speak to foreign government officials about Global Sustainable Energy Independence. We only have one planet. There is no "PlanetB" we can move to if we destroy our environment. Every foreign government official that I have met sees the importance of achieving this task. We can do it, but we must work together realizing that this is not about the black race or white race, Hispanic race or Asian race. This is about the Human Race.

Because of my appointment as Ambassador for the International Human Rights Peace Commission, I have had the opportunity to travel to and speak with thousands of people in Mumbai, India, Calcutta, India, Chennai, India, Jinan, China, and Paris France. Speaking in the top of the Eiffel Tower was a thrill of a lifetime. Receiving a peace award at the Jain Installation in Mumbai was humbling. Receiving an honorary doctorate degree in humanities in Chennai was rewarding, but helping people have a better life with clean energy, better education, a home, food, and healthcare is what makes it worthwhile.

The movement continues to grow with supporters in Spain, France, India, China, Haiti, South Africa, Nigeria, Ghana, Liberia, Switzerland, and all over the United States. We will Rise Up like a Phoenix out of the ashes of a divided world and into the glory of a unified people.

# The 2020 - Rise Up Movement

The Rise Up Movement began on November 21, 2011. It was my goal to grow the movement nationally. My thought process was to work extremely hard by going across the United States. Positive activity will eventually yield positive results. I envisioned early on that one day we would see people all across the United States running for public office under the umbrella of the Rise Up Movement as a band of New Breed Democrats.

As you could imagine, it has been very tough at times. In the early stages no one took my campaign to be serious. Hardly anyone would listen and the media hardly ever paid attention, but I did not quit. I would show up at events with only a handful of people attending to hear what I had to say, but I did not quit. In 2016 I was blocked from the Democratic Party debates even though over 30,000 phone calls went into the DNC demanding that I should be heard, but I did not quit.

In January of 2016 the campaign bus broke down in New York leaving me stranded in the city for a month. The campaign was operating on a shoestring budget and we ended up losing the campaign bus because we could not afford to have it repaired. I was stranded in New York during one of the worst snow storms the city has seen, but I did not quit.

I was promised major financial support from individuals that never followed through leaving the team and myself discouraged, but I did not quit. I had traveled long distances to several events that were supposed to raise funds for the campaign only to see no funds raised, but I did not quit.

I was offered a position in Atlanta that I took only to have the CEO of the company inform me that he was shutting the company down a few weeks after I secured a new home, but I did not quit. I lost two jobs in my coaching profession, and my reputation was drug through the mud, but I did not quit.

I have had failed business deals and failed relationships, but I never quit. I have always chosen to continue to fight for my goals. As I have gone through life, I have learned that it is ok to fail. I have learned that it is ok to fall down, but I have always found strength from within to pick myself up, dust myself off, and continue on towards my goal.

You see the Rise Up Movement embraces those who have fallen. It embraces those who have failed. It embraces those who have fought, but came up a little short. Our movement embraces these individuals because even at our lowest point we can choose to Rise Up. An individual can be focused on a goal and work extremely hard day in and day out to achieve that goal and never be guaranteed success, but if that individual ever quits, that person is guaranteed failure.

Our movement is filled with individuals that choose to win by getting up when they fall. We push forward. It is painful at times, but we march on.

Over the past seven years we have seen the Rise Up Movement spread across the entire nation and into many other nations. I have had the opportunity to speak in major cities across the United States, China, India, and France in front of thousands of people. The movement has grown to a point where government leaders from foreign nations request our presence in their country, and we go. The growth of the Rise Up Movement has become exponential. I attribute this growth to my stubbornness to never quit.

The Rise Up Movement promotes World Peace by accepting all people and promoting Sustainable Energy Independence with improved Education. We only have one planet to live on. There is no "Planet B" that we can move to if we continue to destroy the environment. Sustainable Energy Independence will not only clean up the environment, but it will create millions of good paying manufacturing jobs in the United States and around the world. It will also get the United States out of constant conflict in the Middle East due to our interest in their oil supply.

As a former Educator and founder of the Rise Up movement, I understand the problems we face with our educational system in the United States and around the world. When an educational system falters, society will begin to fail. Currently the United States ranks 36th internationally in Education. We must educate our students at a younger age and longer as well. That is why my plan calls for Universal Childcare. This will educate our children at a younger age, but it will also free up millions of parents to go back to school or back to work. My plan also pushes for free college education all the way to a bachelor's degree. Currently, the United States is the only Western Industrialized Nation that does not have free college tuition. This will change under my leadership as President of the United States. My plan also eliminates the $1.5 trillion in student loan debt, and we know how we are going to pay for it.

We have a major problem as well in the United States with gun violence in schools. My plan, "Vets for Kids" will protect every child in every school across the nation by employing thousands of Veterans to serve as guardians for our children. As with any staff position in our schools, we will screen and train our Veterans to protect our most valuable assets - our children. Yes, I believe in the Second Amendment, and that every law abiding, mentally competent American has the right to protect themselves, their family, and their property.

The Rise Up Movement also takes the stance that the United States is a beacon light for Freedom for many people around the world. Our nation was built on immigrants, and we must always be the country that gives people hope for a better life. I have always believed that you win with People- not things. I have always believed that We should build bridges - not walls. My plan "Service for Freedom" will secure our Southern border by quadrupling our border patrol. We will do this by taking the 20,000 employees that work in the ICE division and transfer them to the border patrol. Once our border is secure, we will allow poverty stricken individuals to enter our country and serve in local, state, or federal government jobs as well as the military for four years. During that time period, the immigrants will learn the English language, learn about the history of our nation, and earn a taxable wage. At the end of the four year period, the immigrants will have earned their citizenship.

Our world has a long way to go to achieve World Peace, but we will get closer to achieving it by keeping our military and economy strong, achieving Sustainable Energy Independence, and improving Education. We have come a long way, but there is still plenty of work to do.

The 2020 campaign trail has been amazing. From the moment I made it official by announcing in front of more than 40,000 people in Atlanta, GA that I would seek the Democratic Party's nomination for President of the United States, it has been an amazing journey. Since announcing, I have had the honor to speak in Phoenix, Las Vegas, Carnegie Hall in Manhattan, the SC Democratic Convention in Columbia, Atlanta, the University of South Carolina, and Little Rock.

All of these successes have come from years of sacrifice, from perseverance, from a burning desire to overcome whatever obstacle is placed in my path. There have been people along this journey that have helped me in ways that can never be repaid. I think of my family, my moms, my friends. Your encouraging words and acts of kindness have inspired me to continue.

The naysayers have also inspired me. In fact, it's the naysayers that have placed a burning desire inside of me to prove that they have it all wrong. I thank everyone that has ever doubted my abilities, spoke down on my chances, laughed at my lofty goals, and discounted me as worthless. You have lit a fire within me to prove you wrong, which I have done and will continue to do.

# The 2020 Campaign

When the spring of 2018 rolled around, it was a given that I would run again for the office of President of the United States. The end of the 2016 campaign had left a bad taste in my mouth. I knew we had a great plan, but I also knew that the establishment of the Democratic Party did everything in their power to keep me hidden from the public. The Democratic Party made it very apparent that Clinton was going to be their nominee, and nothing was going to stand in their way, especially a young candidate that was eager to run circles around Hillary on the debate stage.

It was just a matter of waiting for the right moment to announce that I would run again in 2020. That opportunity presented itself in March of 2018 in Atlanta, GA at the Sweet Auburn Music Festival. This event had over 40,000 people attending, and I was living in Atlanta at the time. Throughout the day different musical artists took the main stage and rocked the crowd. As the day went on, the crowd continued to build, and I was surrounded by my campaign staff, supporters, security detail, and videographers and photographers.

My time on the stage came late in the afternoon and as my time drew close, I had the opportunity to meet Lil

Scrappy backstage. Then I was informed that he would be performing just before I would take the stage to speak. When the organizers told me that I would follow Lil Scrappy, I joked to him that everyone would leave after his performance and no one would stick around to hear me speak. Lil Scrappy came up to me and told me not to worry because he was going to get the crowd fired up for my speech. Well, he did just that. He had the crowd rocking, and at the end of his performance, he gave a huge shout-out to me.

When I took the stage, everyone was still there. They wanted to hear what I had to say. I was asked by a supporter after my speech if I was nervous to speak in front of that many people where I was actually the minority in front of thousands of African - Americans. I thought about the question for a second, and it dawned on me that being a minority in that moment never crossed my mind. I was focused on stepping into my purpose and making sure that my message was on point for every American citizen that was there.

About half way into my speech, I announced that I would be seeking the office of President of the United States and that Mr. Trump did not need to get too comfortable in the Oval Office because I was coming for his seat. When I made that announcement, the crowd of 40,000 people began to roar.

It was official. I had laid it on the line. It was time to get to work. A few months later the campaign trail became very hectic. We did not have much money so I literally drove to a lot of events around the country in my own car. As a lesser known candidate, we made some great strides ending up on the primary ballot in several states including New Hampshire, Missouri, Colorado, Texas, and Louisiana.

I kicked around the country speaking and making appearances at any event that would give me the chance to speak. During the summer of 2019, the debates had begun and twenty of the top Democrats were included in the debates. The first debate was actually two nights because there were too many candidates to debate in one night.

There were way more than the 20 candidates that everyone saw on television, but the ones that received the air time were sitting Congressmen, Senators, Billionaires, former governors, and the former Vice President. I was a lesser known candidate so I had to sit on the sidelines during the debates like a third string running back chomping at the bit for the opportunity to get in the game to get some of the action. I never questioned if I had made the right decision. I was too persistent for that. Some would say I was stubborn. I call it persistency.

On June 22, 2019 the top twenty Presidential Candidates of the Democratic Party were invited to speak at the South Carolina Democratic Party's Convention. Even though I was from South Carolina, I had come to the realization that only the top twenty candidates would be able to speak at the convention. I actually scheduled a speech that same morning in Atlanta, GA to stay busy, and to keep myself from focusing on the fact that I was being shutout of the convention in my home state.

As I drove to Atlanta early that morning to deliver a speech at 10:00 am, my dear friend Tiffany Brown sat in the front passenger seat with her headphones on listening to music. I was listening to CNN on satellite radio. Tiffany took her earphones out and looked at me and said "They are going to call you from the convention today and want you to speak." I looked at her like she had lost her mind. I tried to explain to her how the twenty candidates that were speaking were all Senators, Congressmen, Billionaires, former governors, and the former Vice President of the United States. I told Tiffany that we were fighting to get to that level, and that we would get there one day, but it would not be this day. She looked at me and said "Nope. You're wrong. They are going to call you today, and you are going to speak at the convention." Once again I looked at her like she was crazy as she put her earphones back on to listen to her music.

I did not think much more about it. We arrived at the event in Atlanta, and I gave a speech to about 100 people in attendance. The Creative Society hosted the event and actually broadcast my speech to over 180 nations. I remember thinking how crazy it was that people around the world would drop what they were doing in foreign countries to hear me speak. I had spoken in Jinan, China to more than 30,000 people in attendance and a national television audience. I had spoken to 20,000 people in Mumbai, India and that event was televised nationally in India. Those two speeches reached over three billion people. That is half of the world's population. I had even spoken in the Eiffel Tower in Paris, France and met Lara Jalloh, who went on to be the 2020 Miss Europe. I remember asking myself if I would ever get my opportunity here in the United States.

After my morning speech in Atlanta, I thanked everyone for the opportunity, and I thanked Marina Ovys for allowing me the opportunity to speak to the international audience.

After the event, Tiffany and I went to get something to eat before we drove home. We were standing in line at the restaurant to order when my cell phone rang. It was one of my campaign supporters, Chance Lebron who was at the South Carolina Democratic Party's Convention in Columbia, SC. He was very excited and screaming in the phone for me to get to Columbia, South Carolina for the convention. He had spoken with the state chairman of the Democratic Party of South Carolina and had persuaded him to let me speak at the convention.

I had been fighting for this moment for nine years. Most days I had felt like I was beating my head up against a brick wall, but this day was different. I told them on the phone that I could be there by 4:00 that afternoon, and I was told that I would speak toward the end of the convention on national television.

I looked at Tiffany in amazement and asked her how she knew this was going to happen. She simply said that God told her. I was floored. We immediately left the restaurant and I drove from Atlanta to Columbia as fast as I could. I remember praying that God would keep us safe and that we would not get pulled by the police. We did not get pulled and we arrived with 15 minutes to spare. Two US Marshalls escorted us straight down the center isle of the convention while Bill de Blasio, the mayor of New York was giving his speech. Everyone was standing up trying to understand what was going on and why this unknown person, me, was being escorted to the front of the convention hall. The mayor actually got flustered in his speech because of it.

The US Marshalls got me backstage and I saw several of the candidates in person for the first time. They did not know me so I was pretty much ignored. I remember getting to myself backstage with only a couple of moments before I would take the stage. I bowed my head and said this prayer. "Dear Lord, I thank you for this incredible opportunity. I have fought hard for nine years to have the opportunity to speak to the American people and share my vision for a better America, yet here I am right now without a speech because I had to drive from Atlanta. So Lord, right now

I ask you to give me the words to speak and let your light shine through me for the entire nation to see."

Then I looked up from my prayer and a stagehand looked at me and said "You're Up!"

As I walked up the ramp to take the stage, I started thinking about my mom and dad. Mom Wells was my first speech coach when I was ten years old. She had helped me overcome the fear of speaking in front of a crowd of people. My dad, a minister for 52 years had taught me different styles of engaging the crowd. It was time. I was ready. My speech lasted for about seven minutes. I spelled out my plan and vision for America, and when I was done, 10,000 people were on their feet cheering for me, the in state candidate.

It happened. Now people across the nation knew the deal, and that I was going to be the guy that would never back down, never surrender, never retreat, and most definitely never go quiet in the night.

During the middle of the winter of 2020, I actually slept in my car at a truck stop in New Hampshire for two weeks as I campaigned for their primary. I remember seeing my name on the ballot in New Hampshire along with 33 other candidates. We had come a long way. The strides our campaign made were absurd considering that I was self funding with literally no money, sleeping in my car, taking showers at truck stops, and surviving on crackers. It was absurd, but usually the most absurd make the best stories. This is mine.

# Queen Esther

O ver the past few years I have been awarded the opportunity to speak all over the United States and in several countries around the world. Because of my travels and the technological world that we live in, I have been able to become friends with people all over the world. The network I have built globally has given me the opportunity to see places and experience things that I could only dream of.

Whenever I speak in a foreign country, I always make sure that friends of the Rise Up movement that live in that part of the world know that I will be in their area and hopefully they can come out to my event and support. I have spoken in China, India, and France, and I have met some of the friendliest people I could have ever imagined. The trips to those countries were amazing where I had the opportunity to speak in front of thousands of people, meet with the international media, meet with foreign government officials, and learn the culture.

So when I was invited to speak in Lagos, Nigeria in the summer of 2022, my team began to make preparations for my visit. We always do our due diligence to ensure that the people hosting the event have everything in place, and that their intentions are genuine.

For the trip to Nigeria, we were extremely cautious because of the current situation in their country that can make it dangerous for foreigners.

We received proper protocol, an itinerary, documentation that security would meet me at the airport and be by my side the entire trip. We received invitation letters that were filed with the State Department that stated the address and phone numbers of the hotel where I would be staying. We even saw banners that were made promoting the event where I was to speak in a large stadium in Lagos.

Something in my gut told me not to travel alone to Nigeria. I made arrangements where two of my friends met me. One of my friends, Nigel Trim came from England. He is a virologist and has done some amazing studies on the Coronavirus. Nigel and I have become business partners with his company, Isophene. Nigel, along with a field of top world scientists have come up with a bio defense infrastructure that will shield off any threat of future pandemics. It was our desire to meet with the President of Nigeria during my trip in order to bring the West African nation on board with this plan that would save millions of lives.

I also invited a dear friend of mine that lived in Port Harcourt, Nigeria. Esther Gabriel is not only a citizen of Nigeria and knows the country, but she is also Miss Nigeria 2022 and won first runner-up in the Miss Globe pageant. She is without a doubt one of the most beautiful ladies I have ever seen in the entire world. Esther loves to speak to children, and it was my thought that she would be able to help us with the people of Nigeria.

My gut was right for inviting Esther to meet Nigel and me in Lagos. On the day that all three of us were to arrive, Esther's flight would arrive two hours after mine, but because my flight was delayed, we arrived at the same time. It was Devine intervention that had us arrive at the same time.

Once I landed and went through customs, a security detail with the organizers of the event was supposed to meet me. Everything had been put in writing as far as security detail, the three car motorcade, the Radison Blu where we would be lodging, the location of the event, and much more.

When I passed through customs, there was no security for me. It was just one man and one lady that had been in contact with us for months. His name was Ray Ashenewen. We knew they were the one's organizing the event. Esther immediately began questioning the couple. At the same time she was texting me where they would not know our conversation.

When we walked out of the international airport, there was no three car motorcade. The only vehicle was an old minivan being used as a taxi. The lady got in the rear of the minivan and Ray and the driver sat up front. This left the middle row where Esther, Nigel, and I sat. Even though Esther sat next to me, she continued to text me so that Ray Ashenewen would not know of our conversation.

Esther began interrogating Ray as we drove away. At one point Ray looked at her and asked why she was interrogating him. His answers were not making any sense. Then she text me and said that she did not believe that he was who he said he was and that it appeared that he was trying to kidnap us. Then Ray tried to get us to go to a different hotel instead of the Raddison Blu. I told him no and that our lodging had been filed with the State Department and that if I was not there, they would hunt him down like a dog.

The driver just laughed as he continued to drive to the other hotel where we were told a group of people were waiting on us. Esther text me that whatever happened, we did not need to go to the new hotel because anything could have happened to us. Even though I told the driver to take us to the Radisson Blu, he continued to the different location.

They had us, or so Ray Ashenewen thought. That is when I bowed my head and said a little prayer that went like this. "Mighty God, you control the universe. We need you to intervene NOW." When I said the word "Now" the minivan immediately broke down. It was a busy road and people began to crowd around on the side of the road to see what was wrong with the minivan. At that point, whatever harm was intended for Esther, Nigel, and myself was completely erased.

The three of us made it safely back to the Radisson Blu, which was gated and under security protection. We took a little time in the lobby to try to understand what had just happened. In a nutshell Esther saved my life with the power of God intervening that day.

I made several calls to local authorities and learned that there was no event scheduled and that the entire ordeal was a setup to take me. We never saw Ray and the lady again. It was obvious that they meant to harm us, and when we were able to get to safety, they vanished.

The three of us stayed at the Radisson Blu until we were able to book flights back home. Esther would not leave my side. Now think of this. Who else can say that the most beautiful lady in the world is their hero? Esther is my hero. I owe her my life.

Even though we are on different continents, Esther and I stay in contact. It is my desire to one day be the President of the United States before I am too old to hold the office as some Presidents have been. It is also my desire to bring the world together. Thanks to Esther I actually will have a chance to do just that.

# The Creative Society

B ack in the spring of 2018 I had the pleasure of meeting Marina Ovys in Atlanta, GA. Marina was part of an international movement called the Creative Society. We struck up a friendship, and I began to learn about her movement and she began to learn about the Rise Up movement as well. The Creative Society has members in over 180 nations. Whenever they have a forum, it will be broadcast around the globe and translated in over 150 languages. It has been an incredible journey to watch our group grow to millions of people worldwide.

Many may ask what is the Creative Society. In a nutshell, we stand for human life and see it as the highest value. The life of all humans must be protected as each individual would protect his / her own life. The goal of the Creative Society is to guarantee the value of every person's life. The most valuable thing in the world is a person's life. If one person is valuable, then all human beings are valuable.

We also believe in Human Freedom. Everyone has the right to be a human being. We are all born the same and every person should be free and equal. Every person has the right to make choices as well. The freedom of all people should take precedence. When human rights are put into place, it must not infringe on the rights of others. It is the

United States Declaration of Independence that states "We hold these truths to be self evident, that all men are created equal, that they are endowed by their Creator with certain unalienable Rights, that among these are Life, Liberty, and the pursuit of Happiness." The Creative Society falls in line with the Declaration of Independence.

The Creative Society also stands for Human Safety. I have always been one who would stand up and fight for those who could not fight for themselves. That is called decency. Everyone deserves to feel safe in their own homes and their environment. No one has the right to threaten the life and freedom of any person. We believe that every person should have essential life necessities such as food and water, housing, health care, education, and social security. The advances that are made around the world in the fields of industry and technology should be made for improving the quality of all human life.

Human safety also includes guaranteed economic stability with no inflation and stable prices around the world. This system also does away with income tax. Everyone has the right to attain reliable information regarding public funds, and every person will have access to making decisions for society. The mass media should also work to ensure that their information is truthful and honest.

We also believe that every person has the right to comprehensive development and personal fulfillment. Education should be available and free for all people. In the

Creative Society we wish to see everyone implement his or her creative abilities and talents.

Now most scientists have accepted the theory of Global Warming, but the Creative Society is bringing light to the fact that our earth's core is becoming more and more volatile. Do not just take my word for it. Do your own research and look at the West Coast of Antarctica and the Mariana Trench. We must come together. This is going to be a major problem for humanity. We are going to have to work together globally to defeat this problem.

Our movement also believes in transparency and openness of information for all people. For too many years our people have been left in the dark about major issues that government has to deal with. When there is no transparency, coverups occur, and this causes scandals. We have seen our share of government scandals. The Creative Society takes the approach that we will all be truthful and transparent. This will eliminate scandals.

We also believe in creative ideology. Let's get back to the times of great inventions and encourage our young people to be creative in looking for solutions to the problems at hand. This will progress humanity to new levels of Greatness.

We also believe in the development of an individual's personality. Every person on the face of this planet is very unique with different gifts, different attributes, and different personalities. We embrace all personalities realizing that this is what makes humanity so interesting.

The Creative Society also believes in true Justice and Equality. Over the doors of the Supreme Court of the United States are the words "Equal Justice Under Law." That sounds really good, but the current justice system is flawed where only the rich can afford to be defended in our justice system. The Creative Society wishes to take steps to remedy this problem where all people are treated fairly including the poor and those who are minorities.

Ultimately the Creative Society would like to see a self governing society. We are not there yet. in fact, we are not even close. This is something we should all strive for where we do what is right all the time. In my humble opinion this is the issue that we should spend the most time trying to achieve because it will take decades to achieve it.

All in all the Creative Society stands for the good in people and coming to a level where we are working with the environment instead of destroying it.

We have a lot of work to do to achieve the goals of the Creative Society, but together we can do it.

As I continue this journey through life, I become more and more aware of the fact that each of us has a very short period of time to make an impact in this world. Our days are numbered from the moment that we are born into this world. Time is of the essence for all of us. Tomorrow is not guaranteed, but our actions at this very moment rest in the palm of our hands. I decided that I would do everything in my power to make this world a better place. We need very serious minded people to step up to take on the challenges we face today. If everyone would take a little time every day to just work on one area that we need to improve in, we could accomplish so much. We have major issues to solve with the climate, homelessness, hunger, health care, Education, gun violence, pandemics, racism, gender inequity, domestic abuse, human trafficking, and the list could go on and on. Imagine if every person would designate one hour a day to make our world a better place. In the United States alone, we would gain over 300 million man hours every day to solve these problems. I have taken a strong stand for all of the people, now I am asking each of you to Rise Up with me.

The 2024 Announcement Speech:

Hello, dear ladies and gentlemen!

Can you imagine how terrifying it is when a massive torrent of water suddenly rushes into your house and leaves nothing behind? When your child is swept away by a flood right in front of your eyes? On his way to school a wave takes him out of the car. How does it feel to realize that you and your whole family must evacuate at any moment, leaving everything you've been living with behind? These are the fears and realities that millions of Californians face right now. Because of a series of abnormal storms, California is in a state of emergency. More than 30 million people are at risk, and entire cities are being evacuated.

Can you imagine your city being hit by the worst blizzard ever? Your house with no electricity, no water because the pipes are ruptured, it's -40 outside, you see nothing but snow, and your car skids on ice, and you can lose control and crash at any moment? That's the harsh reality that residents of the U.S. East Coast experienced to the fullest extent during the holiday season.

And do you know what it means to live in constant fear and expectation that a devastating hurricane or tornado can come to your house at any moment and take YOUR life and the lives of YOUR loved ones? And residents of Florida, Alabama, Kentucky, and other U.S. states know what it's like right now. And these climate disasters have occurred in the U.S. in just the last 2 MONTHS, right before our eyes! Many Americans are caught unprepared by the climate Cerberus, unprotected and unwarned. Our meteorologists are unable to alert us in a timely manner. Our emergency services can't handle the strain. And as we can see, our government does not protect us in any way nor offers any guarantees of safety. People are abandoned to their fate on a massive scale.

And all of us Americans, the one MIGHTY nation, are now in the crosshairs of devastating and unprecedented climatic cataclysms. In fact, we are in mortal danger. So what's next? Are we going to watch as, one by one, U.S. states go under water, are burned by fires, or are wiped off the face of the earth by hurricanes? After all, this is not a problem of one state or another; it is a problem of our entire nation! And I will even say more - it is a worldwide problem. Why?

I had the privilege of participating in the International Online Forum "Global Crisis. Our Survival is in Unity," which was simultaneously interpreted into 150 languages around the world. And I carefully studied the facts and research presented there by an international group of scientists on the cause of accelerating global catastrophes. I know these people, and I understand what they are talking about. These international studies make it clear that what is happening to the climate now is just the beginning. The frustrating progression of cataclysms worldwide indicates that the situation is about to worsen much more rapidly. And this means that more critical anomalies, destructive hurricanes, earthquakes, floods, and unforeseen activations of volcanoes are something that we, as humanity, will be facing very soon in the coming years. We as a civilization have a maximum of 10 YEARS TO LIVE!   Ten years at the most, and that's it! Are you ready to die in 10 years?

Climate has cornered us all today. And clearly, no one is really addressing the issue right now. Trillions of dollars have been spent to combat climate change over the last 40 years. So? Has anything changed? Yes, it has changed. Climate disasters have started to gain momentum. And no method in today's consumer society can solve this problem. Because human life in our world is worthless, it plays no role. Only money and power play a role. What does our science look like now? The protection of the private interests of a SELECT few. And to effectively respond to the climate challenge, we need the most potent unification of minds from around the world. But this is impossible as long as we have wars. In the consumerist format, we will not be able to find a way out. And this all leads us to a tragic end. Either Biden and Putin will kill us soon with a nuclear blast, or we will die in worse conditions because an atomic strike is quick, but the climate will torment us for at least several years while we slowly die off.

During a race for the presidency of the United States, you will see all the candidates promising you to end crime, inflation, unemployment, child homicide, migration, and climate change. But in fact, no one will ever be able to end it in the current consumerist format. The wars will continue, the violence in society will only increase, and you will continue to be robbed and made poor. Why? Because in the modern consumerist format of society, there is always someone who benefits from it! There are always those whose power is above the people. No one will be able to end this mess in the economy or domestic politics. NO ONE CAN, because they don't know how! BUT I KNOW HOW! So I stand before you today to announce my candidacy for President of the United States of America. And you know why I am confident that I will succeed? Because my platform is the Creative Society - it's your bright, free, secure future. And it's one that millions of people around the world already support. And I will not be building the Creative Society alone. I will be building it not even with millions but with BILLIONS of people!

What is a Creative Society? It is a society where Human Life is valued above all else! Where there is no power of the few over the majority, where all power belongs to the people. It is a society where there are no enemies and no wars. And so only in a Creative Society is it possible to unite the world's scientific potential and provide a solution to the climate problem and guarantee the safety of Americans and all people on the planet.

Unlike the other candidates who will resist this, who go into a position of power to manipulate, rule the nations, and save their own asses, I go to save humanity. You can put my words in the bank, and they will yield you dividends. I can end all mess once and for all, end wars, and make the world beautiful, peaceful and prosperous by building a Creative Society. If I become president, you will all live a life you never dreamed of. It's a world that not even science fiction writers have written about! Free energy, free health care at the highest level for everyone, free education, and no taxes for small and medium-sized businesses, no taxes for individuals.

Yes, many people will say it's fantasy and can't be, but I say it's real! I guarantee every American an unconditional

basic income of $10,000 a month! There will be no infla-
tion. And even more than that, I guarantee that once we
move into the Creative Society, all debt will be canceled!
And, of course, there will be no utility bills, no energy bills,
and everyone is guaranteed free housing. The Creative Society is a WHOLE different world, built on the value of
Human life. And because of this, we will quickly fix and
resolve all climate issues. I'm the only one who can do it
because I have the Creative Society behind me.

I have decided to run for president as an independent candidate. Because I can't run from just one part of
the American people. I can't divide the country - I want to
unite it. I am sorry, but right now, in America, party affiliation is akin to religion. If born into a Republican family,
you have to be a Republican. Born into a Democrat family,
you have to be a Democrat, and it can get pretty idiotic
sometimes... Who has not seen this phenomenon where
people stopped communicating and friendships when they
learned they had different political views? I am for a united
party, united Americans, united America, and that says it
all! And I'm all for bringing the nation together, and I'm
all for this being the last election of politicians in America
because there shouldn't be any politicians. They are the ones
who are ruining you and destroying you. No one has done
more damage to you than politicians.

When a politician speaks on your behalf, he is simply manipulating your opinion. And even if the majority

disagrees with him, there's nothing you can do, we elected him, and he does what he wants to you. We can't even punish him. And when you, the people, have power, you are the ones who decide. And that's why I'm running for president, to give you your power back. By supporting me, you're supporting yourself in the first place, NOT SOME CANDIDATE.

Don't give your power over yourself to anyone else. YOU must keep the power, and I will be the guarantor of that! We all deserve to live in a society with self-government that allows us to make our own decisions and determine our own destinies.

I am running for President of the United States of America to give power BACK to Americans. Not to keep it for myself, to take away your taxes, to force you to vaccinate, to force you into debt slavery, and to make as much money off you as I **can.**

I am running for President of the United States of America to give power back to the people and build a Creative Society worldwide.

I am running for president of the United States of America to be the first president of the people and the last president of America. Yes, you heard right, the last president of America. Why? Because I will give all power to the people.

Without a Creative Society, no matter who you elect or appoint, there will still be lawlessness. Corruption will continue to flourish, and political parties will continue to fight each other. Things will only get worse.

Without a Creative Society, what is coming is worse than nuclear war. This truth about the climate you don't know yet. The climate is changing dramatically, the **situation** is worsening very quickly, and it is serious.

Look at the progression of abnormal climate disasters, and those who are wise will see. The world is on the brink of total destruction. My words are worth more than gold right now. All the gold in the world is not worth what I am saying to you today. **Because** it will give you a choice between Life and Death. Life is worth more than gold... And the dead don't need gold. So we have something to trade for: death for **life.**

I could come out like the other candidates and talk about education, better living, and the greatness of America. Americans, frankly speaking, given what is happening with the climate, there will be no America, China, or anyone else in a few more years. No one can do anything about it now, BUT I CAN, and I know how to fix it. The other candidates have only money behind them, and they can't buy off the climate. Our dollars are of no use to the climate **Cerberus.** But I know what to do. I can not just save humanity - I can change the world. That is because I have the truth and all of humanity behind me. I have Creative Society behind me. You can put my words in the bank - if I become president of the United States, I will build the Creative Society.

And that is why I am seeking the presidency of the United States to be the first president **from** the people and not from a party with one interest or another behind it.

I am seeking the presidency of the United State to give you, the people all power.

I am seeking the presidency of the United States to build a Creative Society.

We have a tremendous job ahead of us to do as humanity. Power must go back to the people. There must be no politician **at all after me.** It will be gone, like Ancient Rome. We will only read about it in the history books.

We are building a Creative Society where there will be no mess, no corrupt people, and no freeloaders. There will be peace because there will be the main thing - all power will be in the hands of the people, and the highest value will be the Life of Man. People must govern the world. Only then will there be peace, order, and justice.

Are you surprised that I'm saying this? But it is true! As long as politicians sit on your neck, you will remain their slaves. After all, who manipulates you? Politicians, of course. And no matter whose tune they play to, they are politicians.

Do you know why politicians are afraid to hand over power to the people and tell them it's impossible? Because they're scared of being left with nothing, worried that they, the politicians, like ordinary people, will have to actually work. They will have to get off your back, roll up their sleeves and earn their own bread instead of taking it away from you, using various techniques of manipulation and **deception.**

No matter how hard the government tries to brainwash us about external enemies, it no longer works. Why? I'll give you an example. I will tell you openly: just so you understand, people in America love Putin more than they love Trump and Biden, and if Putin were to run against Biden or Trump or anyone else in America right now, I am telling you openly, Putin would win with a landslide. People in America respect Putin. Do you know why? Because he's a man, a real man. That's why he would win the American presidential election by a considerable margin. Seventy, maybe 80 percent of Americans would vote for him. I guarantee that.

But I want to tell you this, if I were running for president of Russia right now against Putin, I'd be the only person in the world who could beat him. I would beat Putin with the same result as he would win in America against Biden and Trump. Do you know why? Because my campaign is based on the Creative Society platform, which millions of people around the world already support today.

And it will be the same in China. If I put myself up for election against Xi Jin Ping and the entire Communist Party, all of China will be for me! Because the Creative Society gives freedom and equality to the Chinese, they will be provided with everything. The Creative Society will provide for everyone and remove violence and unjustified control.

No more corruption, no more power, no more slavery. No one will rule over people, and the Chinese will manage their own lives. A Creative Society is caring for the individual when the whole society takes care of one person, and one takes care of the entire society. The Creative Society is the future of all **humankind.**

Every normal, adequate person wants to live in a Creative Society. Only those who do not know about it do not support it. If people knew, everyone would support it except for a few idiots who want power over you.

And the interest of ordinary Americans, the interest of America, is for every American to live better than anyone else in the world. The interest of the Creative Society is for everyone to live in peace and prosperity, the way all Americans should live. So we will build a Creative Society all over the world, and we will start here in the United States. Yes, I say all over the world, not just America, because we Americans can't be happy when there are wars somewhere, when children are starving somewhere, and someone is dying of thirst. We are not beasts; we are human beings. We are Americans, and our conscience and honor will not allow us to be happy and free when there is violence and injustice in the world. So our goal is to make the whole world happy, which can only be achieved in a Creative Society.

Because the Creative Society is precisely the life we've all always dreamed of, and the most important thing is our security. It is tomorrow's well-fed, warm, beautiful day with great opportunities for everyone. But for this day to come, I must become president because no one will give you power but me. And no one will fix the climate problem. That's why I'm running, to save humankind. And as president of the United States, I will introduce the Creative Society program to all other presidents. And believe me - I will find arguments to convince them why it benefits them. They will have only two choices: to do what I say or to fall prey to the climate Cerberus.

And I emphasize again that I will be the first president of the people and the last president of America. I'm going to give power back to the people. Only together can we do that. Together we will build a very different world. We Americans will live a MUCH better life. People all over the world will live much better than we did in the best of times **for America,** in the heyday of American **democracy.** Join me, join me in my campaign. It's not really an election for me to be president; it is the election of the Creative Society format by the Americans and all of humanity. This is not the bottom of the barrel of the consumption utopia we are in now. A creative Society is the choice of a much better, safer, more honest, and happier life. And that has to start with America; we are the only ones who can do it. We will restore America's greatness. We Americans, before the climate destroys us, will build a Creative Society in America and around the world!

I've been looking for this all my life. I've always wanted to make our country and the world a better place. And now I have a real chance to do it! **And** I'm going to do it! That's why I'm running for President of the United States, to build the Creative Society and make the whole world a prosperous, safe, and happy place!

Everybody join me! To vote for me is to vote for life!

Vote for Robby Wells! Vote for your Life!

may God bless the people of the world and may God continue to bless these United States.

Rise up!

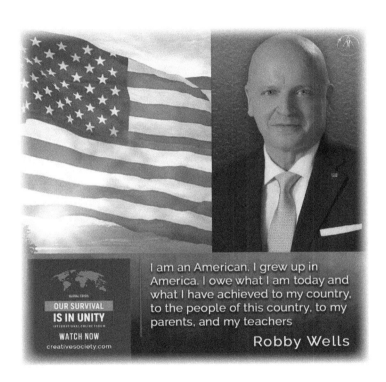

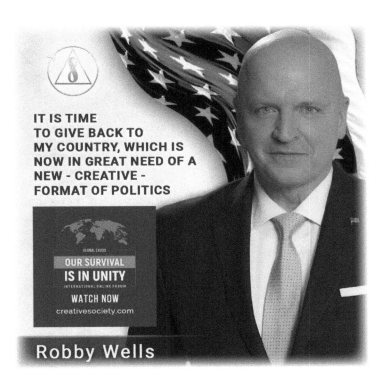

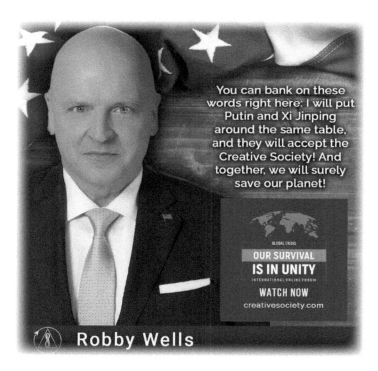

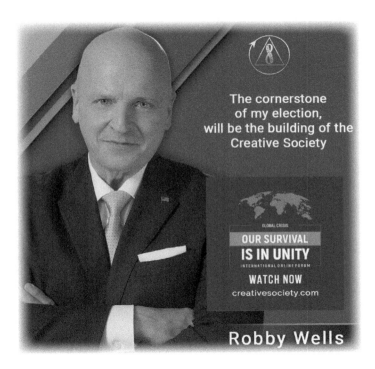

Miami, Florida – February 4, 2022

An Interview with NTV – Russia regarding the Russian / Ukrainian War

The Speech seen in 180 nations thanks to the Creative Society.

Los Angeles, California – September 2015

Jinan, China – April 2017

Atlanta, GA – May 2018

Chennai, India – July 2019

Mumbai, India – October 2017

Mumbai, India September 2017

Family

The Campaign Bus in Savannah, Georgia

L-R: Row 1: Curtis Barrineau, Len Frederick, Robert Wells, Kevin Kendrick, Pat Turner, Eric Eberhardt, Mike Wood. Row 2: Patrick Baynes, Richie Harris, Dwight Sterling, Steve Duggan, Chris Roper, Alden Milam, Brian Pitts, David Adams, Bill Foster. Row 3: William Hall, Robbie Love, Kelly Fletcher, Eric Duffy, David Cobb, Greg Key, Ken Berry, Jeff Raymond

Furman University Football Senior Photo 1989

Furman vs Marshall 1989

Talladega Motor Speedway 2014

Head Football Coach –
Savannah State University

Defensive Coordinator –
South Carolina State University